Womanhood.Shattering False Notions

Eniola F. Omotosho

Preface

When I started writing this book, I did not believe that I could finish it. I actually got the instruction to write the book just after I had turned 17 and I was instructed to finish it when I turned 19; the end of my teenage years. This book is something that I hope God will use to bless both the old and young.

My approach is quite unusual. This book is not strictly for matured women. It starts "young" and then grows and gets deeper. This way, the reader is able to grow with it as well. It is a book for the young, the not-so-young and matured readers. In particular, matured readers are able to see where they have made mistakes and, by God's grace, start to make amends where they need to.

For younger readers, the book is like a guide book, providing directions on what they should expect and how they can cope with these by the guidance of the Holy Spirit. It will take them back to Christ who is the ultimate standard. This book aims to make sure that the true misconceptions of womanhood are identified and outlined; then tackled with the truth of the word of God. This way our young women are able to have an example; they are able to grow into beautiful gems that will cause immense change wherever they may be.

This book has been a learning curve for me because as I wrote I was able to learn and discover new things and pull out things in me that were unknown or rather had been hidden by God until the appointed time. God has taught me so much within this short period of my life and I will always be grateful to Him as I continue to learn at his feet.

This book will not just focus on the age brackets that are listed. Every reader, irrespective of age, background or orientation will find something to hold on to. The reader is therefore encouraged not to take it at face value but to look deeper and understand these different stages of growth; spiritually, emotionally and psychologically as a woman.

Contents

Introduction

I trust and pray this book meets you in perfect peace and soundness of mind. I pray that the peace of our Lord Jesus Christ will rest upon you as you read this book and I also pray that you will be richly empowered and greatly enlightened as you flip through the pages of this book. As a young woman also, it's a great pleasure to write to you and to share the musings of my heart. I believe that there are so many mistaken notions when it comes to biblical womanhood and the church. The aim of this book is to address these erroneous conceptions and shed light on the grey areas through the scriptures.

This book will cover many areas such as identity, desire, modesty, character, godly relationships and the likes. These areas will be dissected and by the grace of God the mistaken beliefs will be rectified. This book will be in three sections titled 'Cherub', 'Prime' and 'Ripe'. This is because I want to be able to identify the misconceptions in each stage of growth into a woman as the Lord will permit and lead me.

A cherub is an angelic personality. This may also denote a beautiful and innocent person; a child-like individual who is pure and untainted. The reason I titled this section 'Cherub' is because we are first young girls before we are young women. There are so many things that we are taught wrongly or are not taught at all about this precious stage of our lives. It is important to scrutinise what we have been taught so that we can correct where possible and also teach the next generation of women. So I will deal with the foundations such as, what does it mean to be a young Christian girl? How can I develop self-worth? What is the meaning of purpose? Prime, as a noun, refers to the time of early womanhood; the prime of youth. I believe this is between the ages of 18 and 22. However, this is not solely when it begins or ends but an estimate to aid understanding. As a matter of fact, a woman can be 30 and still be in the prime of her womanhood. Maturity starts in the mind and is a product of many factors.. This is usually when this female feels free to leave the nest which is usually her parents' house or when God starts to give her wings to fly. This is when she begins to make decisions that can build or ruin her if not made wisely and by the guidance of the Holy Spirit through godly counsel. I will deal with things such as mind-sets on modesty, godly relationships including friendships, mentorships etc. Also what desires are biblically correct? How is my character matured? All these and more will be discussed and the misapprehensions will be picked out. As I said earlier, this stage is also not limited to the age bracket but it's applicable to women of all ages who are in this stage of budding in their womanhood.

'Ripe' refers to the highest stage of growth, development or excellence. Usually, this is from the mid-twenties onwards, but as I mentioned earlier this is only an estimate and it all starts in the mind. A woman who is 40 can still be in the prime of her womanhood.

When the misconceptions in these different stages have been identified, by God's grace I will be able to suggest ways in which they can be overcome by the reader and by the church. Lastly, this is also applicable to all women of all ages who are in this place of readiness in their maturity in womanhood.

My Testimony

$\mathcal{I}$ grew up in a dysfunctional family; by that I mean that my family was intact but was violence-ridden. My dad was very abusive. I heard that he stopped smoking when he found that my mom was pregnant with me. I remember the various times he hit my mother right before my very eyes. Little did I know that he was struggling with the spirit of pride. I grew up and saw more and more violence but never did I for one day question the love he had for my mother. Well, I believed that that was the correct way to love. I occasionally received slaps from him here and there. It was often due to me sharing some food with the neighbour's children, or if I was doing my school assignments incorrectly. I wondered why he would first hit me before explaining. Is it not normal to explain to the child why their grammar or maths assignment was incorrect before yelling down their ears? I had a very flawed view and understanding of what a father's love was. Once in a while, my dad will sing to me but the next minute he would be angry and yelling at me. Therefore, I was a very confused little girl. The only place that I could run to for help was to my mother and she always showered me with love. No matter how she felt, she never took it out on me. However, I still wanted my father's love and attention. From the age of five, I started to get involved in sexual activity. I remember when I got sexually involved with a boy who was between the ages of 10 and 13. By the way, this happened at a 'family gathering' back home in Nigeria and lasted about a month. I still wonder why it was that long. . I remember we would go into a room and I would get naked before him and give him full access to every part of my very little body. I remember him doing all sorts to my body whilst I lay still on the floor and 'got involved' when I felt that he was getting bored. Lord! My mind was so perverse. I knew what we were doing was somehow wrong, but I did not understand to what extent. I remember being so manipulative over him. I'd force him to kiss me and touch me. Sometimes I'd direct his hands and when he didn't do as I told him, I would threaten to report him. I was around him for about a month until I moved back to my hometown, Lagos.

When I got back to Lagos, I started to attend school and everything was 'normal' for about two years. By the way, my 'normal' was violence from my dad, being forced to watch the news and learn about politics, drinking coffee and spirits with my dad every other night and obviously attending school. The year I turned seven, I made this new friend. She told me about this guy that she really liked in her neighbourhood and how they had been kissing and in her own words "we have been having sex too" That was the first time I'd hear the word 'sex', so I had no clue what it meant. Let me add that she was much more mature than her age. She carried herself like a teenager and spoke of things I had never heard of. I believe this was because of her having three younger siblings, so she had to mature quickly. If she did not tell you her age, you'd think she was 13, also puberty had come quite early for her. She went on to tell me about her boyfriend who was about 6 years older than we were. He was 13 years old. She went into detail on how they went about their sexual acts and from there we became very close friends. I remember my aunty buying me a diary and I used this diary to record whatever she taught me. She taught me the act of masturbation; however, we were not aware that it was called that at that time. After a few 'trials' on each other and on myself, I told her that I did not really like the act. Most times, we wished we could sit in-between the legs of our male teachers just so that we could feel their privates. Our minds grew more corrupt day by day. I recall the time she earnestly begged me to go home with her so that I could meet her boyfriend, as her parents were not at home. In addition, I was seven going on eight. I decided to go with her and informed my dad that I was going to stay with her for a few hours after school so we could do our homework together. On getting there, I met her boyfriend who asked me if I had ever had sex before. I said no. He went on to ask if I would like to give it a go. At that point, so many thoughts were racing through my head, but the main thought was I'd be dead if my parents found out. It took me a while to answer but I refused the offer. Few minutes later after we had eaten, my friend and her boyfriend said I cannot leave without 'playing a little'. So the three of us got naked and fondled each other for about an hour and then I departed from her house.

During one our 'acts' in school, we'd usually wait till an hour after school and hide behind the class room under the tables to do what we wanted to do. One fateful evening after school, we were caught by a teacher. She reported us to the head teacher and my diary was found. We were beaten with sticks in front of the whole school during assembly. My dad was called in, but he never said much about it.

Fast forward to an unfortunate event that led to my father having to take me back to my mother's place of work which was a different state entirely in Nigeria. This unfortunate incident happened and my father decided that he was going to unleash his anger on me. My mother had come down to Lagos for my cousin's birthday and planned on returning to work that same day. My father was aware of this and had expected my mother to come home after the party to drop me off and say goodbye to him.

Unfortunately, my mother was running late and would miss her bus if she had to go home and say goodbye to my father. About four hours later, my father stormed in to his sister's house demanding to see my mother and me. I quietly informed him that my mother had returned to work and was unable to come and say goodbye to him otherwise, she would have missed her bus. He angrily slapped both of my thighs. The burning sensation and the marks of his ten fingers on my laps, got tears rolling down my cheeks. He aggressively dragged both of my arms and pulled me out of my auntie's house.

Little reflection moment: This is where my hatred for men began. I just hated the fact that my father had moved from physically abusing my mother to physically abusing me. That night this seed of hatred was planted and watered.

The next morning at 5am my father got me ready and we got on a bus to my mother's place of work (Ogun State). On getting there, my father claimed that he had a political meeting in another state (Ondo State) and because of that, he will have to leave me at the generator room which was about 10 minutes away from the school kitchen where my mother worked as a supervisor. Please bear in mind that my mother was unaware that he was bringing me to her workplace. Fortunately, my mother's colleague saw me and brought me to my mother. My mother was very furious when she saw me, her anger later became tears when she fully realised what my father had done. In her words 'He has pulled the last straw'.

That evening my mother made it known to me that I was going to be staying with her friend who was a mother to three boys; her eldest being three years older than I am while the other two were younger than me. Everything was alright until her son started making 'advances' at me; by this time I was 8 going on 9. He started quite subtly but as time went on he became increasingly aggressive about his pursuit of my fragile pre-puberty body. I guess his hormones were raging within him. Unfortunately for me, there was a night I came out of the shower and was about to wipe myself dry without knowing he had hidden in an obscure corner of the room which we shared with his brothers and mother.

He subtly took off my towel and with force threw me on the closest mattress and in no time I found his hands all over my immature buttocks cheeks. As he was about to slid his fingers into my private parts, the house help stopped him by shouting into the key hole. She had been watching all along. During that time of sexual interaction with him, I was quite numb and wasn't sure about what I should be feeling. This was demonstrated in the way I laid still whilst he did what he did. Unluckily for me, this had come across as consent from me to the house help who latter reported the case to his parents few weeks later. He denied that he used forced on me and obviously the witness, witnessed against me. Though we both got punished, I felt like I was not being listened to and it fuelled the rejection that I was already experiencing.

A few months after this, my mom adopted my first sister. No too long after she was adopted, we started to get involved in sexual activities. It all started innocently as we played the mommy and daddy game. However, we soon started to fondle each other's private parts while playing mummy and daddy. Thankfully, I believe the Holy Spirit started to prick at my heart and I started to feel bad about the things we were doing and I begged that we stopped. However this had already sown thoughts of practicing homosexuality in me. Obviously, I didn't know that's what it was called. I just wanted to have sexual relations with females. Then came along my mom's friend's son, who happened to be my sister's cousin. He too began to make advances at me. Indeed, he almost raped me on two occasions. Thankfully I was able to get out of the situation quickly. The first occasion was on the night before my 9th birthday. The second occasion was at a mutual family friend's house. He had locked me in and held me down firmly but I was able to kick him off and run out before he could have his way with me.

18 months later, I moved to England. I was very excited because I had always wanted to visit the country where my mom was born. It was also meant to be an escape route from all the things I had been going through back in Nigeria. On getting to England, I quickly got involved in the watching of porn. I did not masturbate as I never felt comfortable with the idea, but I found comfort in watching porn and more specifically when it involved a male that looked a good number of years older than the

female participant. I'd do this weird thing of putting myself in her shoes and wish I experienced this kind of attention from an older male. Eventually, I did get this attention from a guy who was 6 years older than I was, I was 14 at this time. We entered into a relationship because he felt that I acted more matured than my age. Unfortunately that relationship ended on a bad note and I was left heart broken. It stared to go downhill when I found out that he was cheating on his girlfriend with me. In other words, according to the lingo of this generation, I was his 'side-chick'. Anyway I found this out and, being the 'witch' I was, I manipulated him into breaking up with her which he did, but obviously his heart was not with me.

My life was all messed up and I was going downhill fast. Thankfully I experienced salvation when I was 15 and the Lord asked me to break this relationship off. I was not ready to do that because he was the only male that gave me the attention I desired even though he was not even a Christian. So I asked him to change his religion and become a Christian but he objected and said we could get married and I would still practice Christianity, but I knew that will not run with God. So after several fruitless efforts to get him to accept Jesus, we finally parted ways six months before my 16th birthday. It was a very painful break-up but I don't know where I got the strength to get through it and move on. Though this is not detailed, it shows how much of an amazing God I serve and love.

Before I introduced Jesus into my heart, I had a misunderstanding of what being 'female' was all about. Seeing my mother being abused by my father, made me question whether I'd ever want to be a wife one day or whether I even wanted to grow up to be a 'woman'. Well, I never really understood what that term meant anyway, except for the basic assumption that a female is a person who does not have a penis in-between her legs. Growing up as a female was not easy. I had lots of attention from males who were twice or more my age. At a point, I began to find myself craving that attention. It reminded me of when my dad carried me on his lap and called me his adorable little angel. That feeling of warmth, love and attention is what I longed for. Some people might be quick to jump to a conclusion and say, 'but why didn't her mother care for her?'. Yes, of course she did. See, she went to church four times a week; she was in a department, serving with all her might. However, the sad truth is that she was not in harmony with the Holy Spirit. She was spiritually blind. She was not imparting into me, as she had an identity crisis too. I could not understand myself and understand why I was created. By the time I got into my teenage years, I had developed a hidden hatred towards males because of the sexual abuse I had been subjected to. I was exposed to the world of sexual immorality. I was exposed to porn, I lusted after the opposite sex, I had dreams of having sexual intercourse with grown men, and I had lesbian tendencies. I lacked confidence, misinterpreted self-worth, craved attention and love and suffered in silence. Praise to God, He found me on 29 October 2011 at the age of 15. I fell in love with my maker, my creator, the lover of my soul. Finally, someone had come to my rescue! I am free from, depression, heaviness, low self-esteem, and all the baggage were off my shoulders. He began to teach me to love myself, love others and love Him even more.

I am sure you can relate to at least one of the things I mentioned earlier. Sometimes we get annoyed at the older females that are in our lives, most especially when they go to church. They tell you everything you need to do to be a "good Christian girl" but cannot see beyond the mask you are wearing. I wonder where discernment has disappeared to in the body of Christ. They are also blinded by the ways and the system of this world. It is vital that as young women ourselves we break this vicious cycle and make sure that we do not make the same mistake with our daughters as our parents have done with us. We need to understand that God's grace is sufficient for us to break this repetitive cycle of hurt, identity crisis and self-worth issues.

Re-Defining Woman

Introduction

Proverbs 11:22 –

[As] a jewel of gold in a swine's snout, [so is] a fair woman which is without discretion.

Let's define the key words there.

Swine: a dirty animal; they are always found in mire (dirt, mud etc.). Interestingly, another definition for a swine is a coarse, gross or brutishly sensual person.

Discretion: The quality of being discreet. To be discreet means to show prudence and circumspection. In other words discreet means: having wisdom, foresight, forethought and sound judgement.

Fair: in this context, this word means: pleasing in appearance or free from blemish. So in other words, to be fair is to be physically attractive.

Therefore, from that scripture we can perceive that a jewel of gold will be ill placed in the snout of a swine. Secondly, we see that the following words: 'so is' shows that there is a matter of comparison going on there. Therefore, a fair woman without discretion is compared to a swine with a jewel of gold in its snout. From this scripture questions such as 'Why is a fair woman without discretion compared to a swine with a jewel of gold in its snout?"

The Hebrew word for fair in that bible verse is yâphâh pronounced: 'yaw-faw'. It's a verb meaning a doing word. That is to say, a woman who adorns herself or bestows beauty on herself via clothes, makeup etc. but her MIND is void of virtue and wisdom is seen as a swine with a jewel of gold in its snout.

Why is it crucial for a woman to have beauty and a sound mind?

The bible has several narrations about the lives of some women who had the power of direction. For example: Eve, Sarah, Delilah, Jezebel, Esther etc.

Wisdom and discretion are like two sides of a coin. They are both modes of direction. As the bride (church of God) determines how the world views God, so does the woman determine the image of her home and her non-marital home. Eve directed her husband to fall. Sarah represented the flesh that Abraham gave in to, he slept with Hagar. Delilah directed Samson to his down fall. Jezebel was directing the people of God to sin. Esther directed her husband which led to the deliverance of the Israelites. So a woman who adorns herself but lacks wisdom, foresight, forethought and sound judgement is not only jeopardising the home in which she has been placed; her family home and her marital home, but also the body of Christ. Proverbs 14:1 '**The wisest of women builds her house, but folly with her own hands tears it down.**'

Proverbs 31:30-31 ESV

Charm is deceitful, and beauty is vain, but a woman who fears the Lord is to be praised. Give her of the fruit of her hands, and let her works praise her in the gates

Chapter 1

Femininity? Masculinity?

*F*irstly, human beings were created in two groups, as men and women. Usually their characteristics are most commonly referred to as masculine and feminine traits. This is because, according to biology, a woman is an adult human female. She has a vagina, more tissue on her chest than a man (breasts). She has the organs needed to bear children, she's usually curvier than a man and she usually does not have visible facial hair etc. This is all due to a higher level of the oestrogen than testosterone (a more dominant hormone in a man). This is significant because both men and women have masculine and feminine traits. From a broad view therefore, we can say that a man is predominantly masculine, and a woman predominantly feminine. There are always exceptions, and this is why not every woman will naturally desire what is considered a feminine inclination, nor a man a masculine proclivity. However, the dissimilarities between the masculine and feminine are great and immense. Therefore, these differences affect the way men and women think, feel, speak and act. The differences are psychological, emotional, physical, spiritual and intellectual. Then, while we may be a combination of both these masculine and feminine traits, at the end of the day we are either a man or a woman. Our differences are not meant to cause a distance between us, but to bring us closer together, to complement one another and bond as we become points of celebration, not separation in respect and honour for each other's gender.

The greatest difference between a man and woman—or, more appropriately, between the masculine and the feminine, physically speaking, is the seed of a man. It is the commencement of all life, the base. In its absence, no life will ever be able to come into existence. It is invisible to the naked eye. However, it has potential, incredible potential, but it cannot develop or grow or form by itself. Physically, the reproductive organs of a woman are internal, whereas that of a man are external. This ability to internalize and to develop within is, once again, understood as something much more than merely physical. One of the clearest indications of this is the difference between the obligations of men and women according to scripture.

The ability to receive the potential of the seed and cultivate it into something tangible and meaningful is beautiful. While it is not compelled to do so, it wants to do so and in most case the carrier (woman) chooses to. It is a situation where each is dependent on the other to create a reality. The seed cannot become anything in and of itself.

In actuality, or on the most physical of realms, a woman cannot produce seed, and a man cannot house or give birth to a baby. But, while the physical is in many ways the lowest and most external of all levels, it is nonetheless the world in which we live, and the most tangible to us. The physical creation of a baby is the most insightful and perpetual symbol of the love and the bond between a man and a woman.

Let us go back to the Garden of Eden. We see in Genesis that God created MAN, then it goes on to say that MALE and FEMALE he created them in Genesis 1:27. The word created there is 'bara' meaning to create to bring something that wasn't into existence. Then later on in Genesis 2:7 we then see that God formed man. The word formed there 'yatsar' means to form, to frame, to squeeze into shape'. If something is to be squeezed into shape that means it has already been created, it's just being fashioned, and purpose is being assigned to it. We see from previous verses that the Lord wanted someone to till the ground because there was crop and herb in the earth that had not yet grown (Genesis 2:5). Therefore God caused rain to fall and formed man to till the ground. Now after that we see in verse 9 that the Lord then caused all these beautiful trees to grow, to form. Then we go on further to verse 18 where the Lord now sees that it is not to the benefit of man to be by himself. Thus God made(fashioned, squeezed out, appointed) a helpmeet for him. We then see that the Lord out of the same ground formed (yatsar) beasts and he brought them to Adam to name. He named them all but did not recognise them as his helpmeet. God brought these creatures that he had formed to Adam to 'see' (raah- inspect, perceive) what he would call them. We can perceive from this that God was trying to see what Adam will call them but more specifically if he would identify any of them as his helpmeet. The root word for helpmeet is 'azar' and that means: to help, to succour, surround, protect or aid). Furthermore, verse 20 connotes that God probably got concerned that Adam had not found his helpmeet. This therefore caused God to send him into a deep sleep and took one of this ribs, closed up his flesh and I am guessing He then let Adam wake up. Then he formed a woman and then brought him to Adam as he did with the other creatures. However, this time Adam knew that this was the 'bone of his bone and flesh of his flesh'. We also see that he then called her woman; he called her this because he believed that she was taken out of man! Adam could identify her, and where she came from.

So from this we can pick out that a woman was created with the primary purpose of being a companion and help to man. By man I mean mankind because when we look at man in the verses above it is translated to mean human/mankind. Many have argued that women should not be seen as lower than men and that they should be seen as equal and I do agree with that. However, this is where we get it wrong. Women view their role as one that is degrading and unpleasant, yet it is so powerful that the undermining of it brings great discomfort to mankind. Kofi Annan said that 'There is no development strategy more beneficial to society as a whole- women and men alike- than the one which involves women as central players'. This is so true because from the Garden of Eden we can even see that the Lord said it's not good for man to be alone, that man needs a helpmeet; a support system. It vital that the society, most especially the Church, begin to understand the value of women and the need to make sure that they are fully functioning in their God-given callings. When women begin to manifest their ultimate purpose as helpers in their own unique and diverse ways, we will begin to see change that will not only stay in the church but will overflow into the world.

Chapter 2

Hmm...womankind?

The misconception surrounding womanhood is enormous. What is a misconception? According to the dictionary it is a view or an opinion that is false based on faulty thinking or understanding. A misconception is just a false opinion. It is the product of a mind that is faulty or an understanding that has a shaky foundation. It is important that our perceptions and our understanding are not defective. This is one of the reasons why we have many misinterpretations of biblical womanhood in the body of Christ. There are so many opinions on what womanhood should be. Quite ironically there are many writings on it, addressing what is expected of a woman as she grows in womanhood. There are many expectations that are placed on her without first understanding her as a person before trying to instil the responsibilities of her gender. We need to be careful that these misinterpretations do not box up our women and cause them to feel caged in and unable to express themselves in the way God has called them to.

There are many lies regarding what true womanhood is. It has caused a lot of confusion amongst our women in the church, causing them to be moved by every wind of doctrine. Some argue that womanhood is objecting to "dependence" on a husband/man and climbing a corporate ladder in the place of work, government, or some other endeavpour. Others say that womanhood is doing work at home only, whilst some say that womanhood is defined by not wearing chic clothes, make-up, jewellery, etc. Some define womanhood as bearing children, and sometimes how many children one has. This has therefore caused women to chase a vague and hollow identity and dream. It is quite unfortunate that most of our women can't seem to embrace who God made them to be according to the Bible.

It is imperative that women give womanhood a definition that is not based on the culture they were brought up with or they find themselves surrounded by. Similarly, the definition should not even be based on what goodhearted Christians might state but rather on the Word of God. On many occasions I have heard ridiculous things regarding womanhood such as womanhood is knowing how to 'treat boys'. Yes, I am just as dumfounded as you are. That was what a female adult youth leader asked me when I asked her to teach on biblical womanhood to the females in her youth group. Agreed that it might be a part of biblical womanhood, however I have to emphasise that it's a very small section; as a matter of fact, I will call it a sub-section.

Womanhood is not merely a slogan that is worn

as a badge for those who have reached a certain age. It is the development of a God-fearing female who has wholeheartedly decided to accept the call of God on her life as an individual and as a woman. Womanhood is not strictly limited to age, however it should start to be encouraged when a female is almost at the end of puberty. This is so that she can start to recognise that she needs to start taking cautious God-ordained steps as she prepares to 'leave the nest'. It is imperative that her loved ones begin to encourage her to start to seek out God for herself. This will aid the development of a healthy independence.

Womanhood is in stages, just as maturity is. There is no defining/glorious moment when one reaches the peak of womanhood. Every stage of womanhood has a beauty of its own and every godly expression of it should be appreciated and encouraged. This brings us to the main question: 'What exactly is godly womanhood?' Well this is my answer. We see that the first duty of a woman in the bible is to be a help meet. This is a huge responsibility. So therefore, womanhood is the time in which a female comes to the realisation that she is no longer a child. She puts away childish things, a child cannot be a help meet. Children require and demand more than they give. When a female comes to that realisation that she's to live her ultimate godly purpose of no longer demanding but helping, she then begins the process of womanhood. She is then called a woman.

There are many ways in which a female can begin to express godly womanhood or shall I say femininity. The most obvious one is marriage and this is a beautiful gift that the Lord has granted unto humanity. It is amazing that a man can leave his father and mother's house to cleave to his wife so that they become one flesh (Genesis 2:24). However this is not the ultimate way in which a woman can express her femininity and live womanhood to the fullest. One of the primary ways in which a woman first starts to express her femininity and womanhood is in her first home, her immediate family home. Sadly, most women do not get the opportunity to experience the beauty of a 'complete' home. As a result of this she is not able to express her femininity because she is not even taught what it is. Likewise, women who grew up in a 'complete' home but still lacked the atmosphere that is required for a child to grow healthily into a stable independent adult may find it difficult to express their femininity and womanhood in the way ordained by God. As a result it is quite tasking for these women to adjust later in life. Nevertheless, thank God for Jesus, He makes all things new!

Another place in which a woman can express her femininity and womanhood is in whatever sphere of influence she finds herself; be it at school, university, work, church or even in a shop. Once women begin to take on the mind-set of 'it's not good for man to be alone' they will begin to see the need for their input in society and that will also encourage them to want to be a source of companionship to those that might need it. Women are nurturers and this is evident in Genesis 2:24 because the male is encouraged to leave HIS father's house to CLEAVE (cling) unto his wife. To nurture is to be able to incubate, to gestate, therefore women are incubators, they surround and they are the bond of the home. We see this internalisation characteristic for the first time when she was formed. She was taken OUT of man. We also see in Genesis 3:20 that Adam calls his wife Eve (Chavvah) and the root word for that means 'life-giver, to tell/declare, to breath'. Furthermore, we see in that same verse that he calls her mother of all living. The word 'mother' means 'strong water', 'bond of the family' in Hebrew. It also means 'parting, point of departure or division'. So, we can see here that it is a very good symbol of the internalisation of a child in a woman's body. The strong water symbolises the amniotic fluid that keeps the living safe and alive in her and also the umbilical cord representing the bond she creates with the living, lastly, the cervix the point of departure, this is where the living departs from one dimension to another, when it reaches full term. How amazing and intricate is our God!

Chapter 3

Where did it all go wrong?

So where did it all go wrong? Our first instinct will be to say that things went wrong when Adam and Eve ate the fruit in the Garden of Eden. This is true and as a matter of fact this was when the whole of man-kind departed from fellowship with God. Now, we thank Jesus for being the initiator of the new covenant in which we are now reconciled to sweet fellowship with the God-head bodily. However, even under the new covenant it is true that women are still oblivious to their highest calling after being the bride of Christ. The church is still very religious in the way it views womanhood. It limits it all to a cute smile, knee length skirts, long sleeve top, modest makeup and jewellery. Whilst all these can be nice and complimentary, it is easy to get lost in the idea that a gentle and tranquil spirit is in what a woman wears. This is a VERY controversial topic. It is important to know that most women now camouflage behind that image, which reads 'gentility'. Therefore it is important that in the hope of achieving this image we do not raise up young women who might not fit into that box to end up feeling alienated and cast out. It is important that we all understand God's mind when he created woman. When we begin to look at scripture through those lenses we will be able to uncover the beauty of womanhood.

We cannot say this is exactly where it all went wrong, however we can say that once humanity fell from the presence of God both male and female lost their sense of purpose. It has gone downhill ever since. Both manhood and womanhood has been attacked ever since the fall of humanity. Just like Dr. Myles Monroe will say 'When the purpose of a thing is not known, abuse is inevitable'. I concur with that regarding womanhood. As a result of lacking an understanding of the purpose of a woman, it is inevitable to abuse her and her identity.

Often times we argue that "times have changed" so the definition or the purpose of a woman has changed too. I beg to differ, reason being that the purpose of a woman/the definition of womanhood has changed rather than evolve. To change is to become different while to evolve is to develop gradually. Rather than evolving, we have totally changed the rules and made it what we want or dare I say allowed it to suit our ever evolving sinful desires. Now a woman is no longer seen as a helper but rather as a sex symbol, a slave, a 'man' wannabe, a doll, a machine etc. We have two cultures of womanhood, the very degrading and pessimistic culture and the overbearing and officious culture, where women are pressured to behave in a certain way and are put on pedestals. Both cultures can be very extreme and tiresome. It requires a great deal of courage for women these days to function in their God given purpose and PERSONALITY. The reason why I have capitalised 'personality' is because, most especially in the church, women are expected to be quiet and tranquil. This is excellent but it can sometimes be so overpowering that most women who are bubbly and outgoing are left to feel boisterous or are too forward. They are told to 'tone' down their bouncy personality and to act like a lady. Now don't get me wrong, I am in NO way encouraging a lousy character or one that does not have self-control. What I am expressing is that some women feel as though the church focuses more on the conduct of women more than the value of women. Despite what we say we believe about equality, the church tends to focus its (not always biblical, mostly cultural) prescriptions for behaviour on the female half of the congregation. Most of the time it's 'don't do this and do that', 'do this and you'll get this', 'don't do this and this will happen to you.' Although I earnestly hope that someday Christians worldwide will settle on one shared code of conduct (which, most conveniently, we hope will be the one we already align with which is the word of God). The truth is that we're going to keep disagreeing. This is because majority of these codes of conduct are based on cultures and very little on what the Bible says. So while we continue to wrestle with the role of women, what they should do, how they should do it and when they should, we should not forget to speak and discuss the value of our women.

Women are helpers to mankind who express this in many different ways. We should encourage our girls to love God and mankind and to see all they do as ministry unto God. Their desires should not be suppressed or discouraged as long as it does not go against scripture and the person of the Word of God, who is our Lord Jesus Christ. The woman who feels led to be a housewife should in NO way feel bad for her choice; likewise the woman who wants to pursue politics.

We rarely face issues honestly until they're right in front of us; this is bad because the younger women have become good at hiding how they feel about this issue especially in our local churches.

Older vs Younger

As a young woman myself, there is one thing amongst others that really breaks my heart. It is the fact that there are very few role models for our young women. Now I am not talking about general role models and people they can just 'look up to' no. I am talking about women that they can imitate as they imitate Christ. There are many occasions where

I have seen strife amongst out older and younger women in the church. It is not meant to be like this. Every young woman needs support and nurturing so that she can be the best she can. The same goes for young women in the church. I believe they have been sub-consciously overlooked and in most cases ignored.

Let us redefine the role of an older woman and that of a younger one! Let's do this._ Our godly and upright older women are a great treasure. They have all passed through the storms of life and they have fought the challenges now facing us younger sisters. They are very mature in wisdom, understanding, kindness, love and service. There is a certain beauty that shines through their countenance. It is the beauty that comes from them letting peace take its full work in them (James 1:1-4). There may still be struggles, but there is mature wisdom to meet it and this makes them so radiant and blissful. They have pushed way the bad memories of the past, while the good memories are cherished. They bring sweet and satisfying enrichment to life as they teach our younger sisters to treasure the sweet memories they create now as it will be a pillar of strength when they look back over the years. . They have also learned to cherish the scriptures and have friendship with the Holy Spirit. They have mastered the art of prayer; their prayers for the most part are prayers of thanksgiving without ceasing. Their words of greetings flow like milk and honey as they touch the heart of those they speak to. Their friendship is a strong staff on which others may lean; they have the strength to carry a nation. What a resource are the women of The Church of Jesus Christ. They love the church of Jesus the Christ and they are not moved by every wind of doctrine. They honour their place in the body; they bring strength and beauty to its congregations. How thankful we are to you, you are loved, respected, and honoured. They are our treasured sisters, we appreciate and honour them. They bring a measure of completeness to the body of Christ. They have great strength, coupled with dignity and marvellous ability. They carry forward the young women when they can and the men with respect and love, with honour and great admiration.

It was the Lord who designated that men in His Church should hold the priesthood. Jesus gave them the capabilities to strengthen the marvellous organisation, the Church and kingdom of God. Though they've made many mistakes and will probably still make some more, I bear witness before the entire world of their worth, grace and goodness, of their noteworthy capacities and remarkable assistances, and appeal the blessings of heaven upon them, in the name of the Lord Jesus Christ, amen.

To our younger women, they are beautiful beyond measure; they glow with the youthfulness of their age. Their smiles brighten up a room full of gloom. Their ever up-lifted spirit coupled with grace is one to be associated with. Their mistakes are beautiful and their weaknesses are treasured. The body of Christ loves and cherishes them. Their hearts are homes to many, as their wombs are a shield for many. We thank them for being them, though in the past they might have raged against wise counsel, many of them have submitted themselves under the teaching and nurturing of the ones that had gone before them. They are highly valued and praised. The Lord will keep them in perfect peace as they grow and allow the rod to mould them.

Love always

Eni x

Chapter 4

Who is an older woman? (Titus 2:2)

So what does it mean to be a godly older woman? First I would say, obviously she is a woman who is physically and emotionally mature. Secondly, she is a woman who holds God in very high esteem. She has journeyed with God through life and is still holding on to Him. She has an advanced understanding of the word of God. She is able to teach, guide and nature the younger generation. She has built godly character over the years of her time with God. She also has some experiences that she can share with those coming after her.

A godly older woman has an in-depth understanding of biblical womanhood. She understands what it means to be a woman of God in this day and age where many things are thrown at women to devalue them. She understands the difference between the conduct and value of a woman. She is able to take in a younger woman and train her in the way of the Lord. She is not lousy or rude, neither is she a slanderer or a gossip. She walks in the spirit at all times and she has the manifest fruits of the spirit. She is modest in her behaviours, speech, and choice of clothing. She speaks with wisdom and grace. She doesn't hide her weaknesses and neither does she caress them. She is willing to be corrected just as much as she corrects. She is humble and patience is having her perfect work in her. Furthermore, if the Lord grants her the opportunity to be married, she keeps her home and prays fervently over her household. She is the watchman of her home, she supports her family in every way possible. She listens to the unspoken needs of her family, internalises them and brings it forth just when they need it; the only way she does this is because she walks in the spirit at all times. She understands the divine order of God concerning marriage and does not fight against this. But rather takes full pleasure in submitting to her husband. She teaches younger married women to love their husbands and to be reverent in behaviour. This woman is an example to her peers and also to those younger than her. In addition, this woman is not moved by what life throws at her, she has learned to lay hold of joy in her trials. She is accountable to God, her husband, her children and other godly women. She is mentored just as she mentors.

Older women are not given a specific age but they are those who are able to disciple the younger women. Given the content of what they are to teach, their main qualifications would seem to centre on spiritual maturity. It is no doubt that biological age provides life experiences and perspectives that are valuable, but the reality is that every Christian woman and girl should consider herself an older and a younger woman. We should seek out women who can encourage and equip us to live for God's glory even as we seek to disciple other women in biblical womanhood. The idea of older women helping to disciple younger women is not just a smart idea someone concocted, and it is not optional. It's a gospel imperative. The apostle Paul writes,

Older women likewise are to be reverent in behaviour, not slanderers or slaves to much wine. They are to teach what is good, and so train the young women to love their husbands and children, to be self-controlled, pure, working at home, kind, and submissive to their own husbands, that the word of God may not be reviled. (Titus 2:3-5)

In light of this passage, let's consider some questions that will help the church sound the call for women to invest themselves in younger women.

Chapter 5

The Titus 2 mandate

The mandate of Titus 2:3-5 is that older women are to disciple younger women, teaching them how to grow in godliness in their distinct and diverse relationships and calling. There are a number of the codes of discipleship entrenched in this incredible chapter that will help us to understand the precise command to women in verses 3 to 5. We will discuss these codes and why they are important. An article I read by Susan Hunt titled: Wanted: *More Older Women Discipling Younger Women*, inspired these codes of discipleship.

Susan Hunt is a mother and grandmother, a pastor's wife, and the former Director of Women's Ministries for the Presbyterian Church in America.

Code #1: The responsibility of the church to equip women

In verse 1 Paul's letter is addressed to Titus, the leader of that congregation. This shows that it is first the church's responsibility to bring this into light. Most women are not aware that this is a requirement because their local churches have not brought it to light. Paul says here that since women training women is an integral part of the church's ministry, Titus must equip the women in his church to do so. Therefore, it is the responsibility of every church leader to see that women are equipped for this calling.

Code #2: The church should teach sound doctrine

It is quite sad though that in some of our local churches world-wide, the members of the body are lacking in sound doctrine. They lack a personal relationship with the Lord and look solely to the leader for their daily bread. Some don't know how to fellowship with the Holy Spirit. So, in verse 1 Paul tells Titus to teach sound doctrine, doctrine that is healthy or whole. Therefore, we can see here that the disciplining of younger women by older women should flow out of and be consistent with the regular preaching ministry of the church of Christ. This discipleship should help women apply sound doctrine to daily life and relationships. If an older woman teaches/disciples out of pain or pride it will not be fruitful in the life of the younger women because it will not be sound doctrine. This is not healthy for the growth of a young woman. What she learns, if not corrected, can alter the way in which she views herself and also the way in which she conducts herself and what she also teaches the women under her.

Code #3: The spiritual union of the saints

Communion of the saints is one thing that can foster the essential relationship that needs to take place between younger women and older women. We see that in verses 3 through to 5, it tells us that discipleship is not just the responsibility of church leaders (see also Ephesians 4:11-16), it also involves the cooperation of the saints, those that are being led. Biblical discipleship is interpersonal. The content of the gospel should be taught in the context of relationships that certify the gospel. Our relationship with God is individual, but that relationship also brings us into community with his other children. Older women have the generational responsibility to share their gifts and graces with younger women. They are to tell the tales of their triumphs as well as their failures and show how their stories are part of God's grand story of redemption. It is important that this is what our older women are doing. They should not hide their failures and short-comings but they should contribute to the community that Christ Jesus wants amongst his church by also being vulnerable and transparent. This encourages the same thing in younger women.

The Titus 2 command is discipleship that guides and nurtures to mature Christian womanhood. It is a mothering ministry. This is evident in Paul's portrayal of his own ministry to the Thessalonians: **But we were gentle among you, like a nursing mother taking care of her own children. So, being affectionately desirous of you, we were ready to share with you not only the gospel of God but also our own selves, because you had become very dear to us. (1 Thess. 2:7-8).** Where there is lack of communion being encouraged, it will be hard for both parties (younger and older women) to communicate and relate, especially in this age we live in. Everyone is busy doing something or too busy being glued to their phones. So it is imperative that local churches aim to facilitate this communion with their church community.

Code #4: The gospel as our stimulus

There is no denying that investing and pouring out into the lives of others is tasking and can be quite time consuming and daunting. For the grace of God has appeared to bring salvation to us all, and this is training us to renounce ungodliness and worldly passions, and to live self-controlled, upright, and godly lives in the present age, waiting for our blessed hope, the appearing of the glory of our great God and Saviour, Jesus Christ (Paraphrased vv. 11-13). Christ has given us salvation to train us, but training takes time, practice and patience. Salvation does not just do the work the very day Christ was accepted into the heart of an individual but rather it takes time for the salvation to be 'complete'. That verse says that it will train us to reject and to practice. This shows continuity UNTIL the appearing of Christ. So because an older woman understands this, she is to be motivated to want to nurture a younger woman.

Christ came and he is coming back. He appeared in grace as a babe and he will come in glory as the King. While we wait for that glorious appearing we are to make disciples, to be fishers of men (Mathew 4:19). It is important that an older woman remains motivated and encouraged by the gospel otherwise she will become melancholic and weary.

Code #5: The gospel is dominant

At the end of this scripture, Paul closes with a captivating notice of the power of the gospel: [Jesus] gave himself for us to redeem us from all wickedness and to purify for himself a people that are his very own, eager to do what is good (v. 14). This scripture shows us the very purpose of why Jesus did what he did for us. Now if scripture advices that we have the mind of Christ doesn't that mean that we should also be ready to give up our busy schedules and create time to help and nurture people in the way of the Lord in the capacity to which He has granted us?

It is true that some discipleship is age and gender specific but all discipleship is to be gospel-focused. It is Jesus who redeems and purifies us. The purpose of this redemption is for a fallen sinner to become eager to do what is good is the radical work of the gospel. This is the reason why an older woman needs to be grounded in the word of the Lord. The result of her investment in the lives of others is not dependent upon her power or experience. It is only the power of the gospel that changes and transforms an individual. What a woman needs to do is make sure she knows the gospel and lives according to it so that her life will be an example and not just her words.

To conclude, the church needs to facilitate this 'ministry'. It is important to understand that spiritual mothering relationships are very diverse and it will be dangerous to box them up as there is not one formula to it. A Titus 2 rapport may be consistent or alternating, involve two people or a group, take place between older women or young girls, but every Titus 2 relationship will be and should be purposeful. Developing this should be a deliberate determination to boost and train another woman or girl to live for God's glory by living under the authority of God's word, and it will train her in biblical principles of womanhood.

It is imperative to understand that this ministry is not a programme but a way of life. However, I do not dispute that sometimes it may take more structured, programmatic efforts to kick-start these relations.

Chapter 6

Letters to an older woman

*T*his is one topic that I am very passionate about as it really does pain me in the heart when young women don't have older women that they can look up to. It is frustrating and quite sad when the young women now have to search for this guidance in media. To be quite frank the problem starts on both ends of the rope. The younger women are not looking for older women to mentor and guide them and neither are the older women. From my personal experience of growing up in the church I have seen a lot of women who I'd say are capable but who failed to reach out to me.

Here are a couple of letters written by young born-again women who have, at a point in their lives, felt like they've been disappointed by an older woman who was meant to be a godly representation of womanhood to them. These letters aim to help open the eyes of older women to see that which the younger ones might feel towards them. This should help foster a new perspective on how the younger women might view the role of an older woman, thus helping the older gain understanding on how to nurture and draw a younger woman close to her.

Three ladies volunteered to share experiences in writing. Thanks to Linda Adeyemo, Whitney Adedeji and Tolu Ijiti.

Letter one

Dear older woman,

I know it's been a while since I last saw you; well since I left church. I hope all is well with you and everyone at church.

I've written you this letter because I've been thinking about that day, you know, when we had the 'talk' but I don't think I ever told you what happened after that, months or even years later, so I think it's time. I don't have the best memory but I believe it was the summer before I went to college, I was 16. We were in the car, the kids in the back, driving through Liverpool Street and I popped the question, I'm pretty sure you remember it quite well as it's not the kind of question you get on a daily basis. I remember that then, I had been thinking that perhaps it was about time for it to happen, I mean I had held on for a good while, everyone else had done it. That alone should entitle me to some form of 'salute', how self-righteous of me, right? So I figured since you had been in a similar situation that you would know whether I should do it or not, if it'd be something that I would later on regret or not. I asked if you think I should go through with it, your response "You might as well, you're going to do it at some point in your life". The exact confirmation that I wanted.

So a few weeks after that day, I did it. It was a

rushed, painful, unpleasant night. The next few times were no different so I questioned my sexuality. I admit, I regretted it all for the next two years. I wouldn't forgive myself or even speak about it. I wallowed in self-condemnation. A month later, I couldn't be in the same room as him, this I couldn't explain, I felt unclean, impure. See, I had placed my identity and my worth in everything external so after I gave away my virginity, I didn't really know what to do or what I was. Over those two years of wallowing, my identity metamorphosed quite a bit, until it became more or less non-existing. They say that: "loss of identity can result in increased levels of generalised anxiety, low self-esteem, depression, a loss of self-confidence, social anxiety, isolation etc." (quote from Counselling-directory) I suffered with all of that.

The main issue that I want to address is that I blamed you. For ages, I was bitter and upset, I thought you irresponsible. I regretted seeking advice from you and was angry at myself for going to someone who had had their own child in their teens. But two more years from then, I thank God because He orchestrates our steps. He knows what has happened, what is happening and what will happen and He used that situation to draw me back Home. He called me from my pit of condemnation and torment into His purifying and forgiving arms. There was a reason for everything He permitted to be said and done. So I want to thank you, that you essentially played a role in my journey back Home. I now know that God didn't ordain His beautiful gift to me to be used outside of the context in which He proposed it. He's called me to a lifestyle of holiness and purity, and I am still in the process of healing. I hope by the time you get to the bottom of this letter, you are not offended but happy for the place that I'm in and where I'm going. I'll end it here.

Linda x

Letter two

Train a child in the way he should go and when he is old he will not depart from it (Proverbs 22:6). My child, never forget the things I have taught you. Store my commands in your heart. (Proverbs 3:1)

Dear older woman,

Having heard multiple stories of your youthful days (your "good" behaviour in times pasts and your dedication to participating in church activities) I would have imagined you were well acquainted with the standard of the Lord. For this reason, it is with much disappointment that I detail my grievances of how you failed me in being the role model I expected of you.

It is true that no man is perfect in themselves however much of my disappointment arising from your evident lack of concern to thrive in pursuing holiness as a woman of God even in your times of difficulty and loneliness.

I acknowledge your efforts in trying to raise a child in such a corrupted world however because of your lack of true-belief in the LORD the atmosphere that you were creating in the home was just as toxic. Scriptures like "the Lord is your strength" became something we merely quoted but didn't believe and growing up like this affected the mind-set I adopted towards God Himself.

Thank you for raising me in the consciousness of Adonai. Truly I believe somewhere in all that religious activity God showed me that there was more to Him. On the other hand, daily waking up to hear much gossiping, slander, bitterness, un-forgiveness and a lack of love and unity falsely portrayed the Gospel of Jesus Christ to me. This set me on a destructive path that I thank God He has changed for me.

A woman of God should be completely satisfied in and with El-Elyon alone, pursuing no other lover but only the kingdom of God and His righteousness. To see the actions of one man could lead you to give up Christ, completely losing trust in the only Hope of humanity, was so normal that I even followed in your steps for a while. This is the most painful bit for me: knowing that following the example of my biological mother would have been my destruction.

I acknowledge your efforts and once again, I know all have fallen from glory. However to become comfortable with man's fallen state, giving up on what Christ died for is where my disappointment really is with you. I have never requested perfection from you. All I have expected from you is for you to try, to be willing to say yes to God even when it proves difficult. That's the only thing I've ever expected from a role model and unfortunately this is where you have wronged me.

Whitney x

Letter 3

Dear older woman,

You are a woman. So am I. You have made mistakes. So have I. The difference is that my mistakes could have been avoided if only you had shared yours with me. I wish you told me about your past relationships so I would have known when to run away. I wish you told me that I am beautiful so I wouldn't have had to look for affirmation elsewhere. I wish you told me you were proud of me so I wouldn't have wasted time trying to please others.... but it's a lesson learnt. Everyone is an example and you happen to be an example of how not to do things but that in itself is a reason to thank God. Having said that, there are some things I admire. I admire the fact that you want the best for me but you've really told me how to achieve it. I admire the fact that you're open with me but only in regard to issues that concern you. I admire the fact that you try because that's all anybody can really do right? I appreciate you. I appreciate your efforts. I honour you as an elder because that is what I am instructed to do but it's safe to say that I won't be following in your footsteps.

Tolu x

Chapter 7

Be a mentor and be mentored...
Titus 2:3-5

$\mathcal{M}$any young women are seeking the wisdom and benefits of mentoring. Titus 2:3-5 specifically targets women's relationship with one another. Paul encourages the young pastor Titus to identify qualified older women who could, and should, teach and model godliness to the younger women in his church body:

"Likewise, teach the older women to be reverent in the way they live, not to be slanderers or addicted to much wine, but to teach what is good. Then they can train the younger women to love their husbands and children, to be self-controlled and pure, to be busy at home, to be kind,

and to be subject to their husbands, so that no one will malign the word of God."

Countless young women in the body of Christ eagerly desire such a mentor. Someone who will help develop godliness in them as a woman in their own right. However it has proven difficult to find an older woman willing to step into that role. Sometimes this is as a result of the older women feeling unqualified, panicky, and fearful of over-committing. This is typically because they do not know what it means. They do not know how far is too far, where and how to start and stop, what the content and structure of this mentoring will be. This can sometimes make older women shy away from this beautiful duty. What is really needed for a kick start is a heart devoted to God, experience in life and a love for people. Women who have these characteristics, can often mentor someone else. Often the reason I hear from older women who have shied away from mentoring is that they feel as though the younger women are 'smarter'. However, I beg to differ. Reason being, due to the times we live in, the younger generation now have more of a voice due to the wide range of things they are exposed to from their tender ages, thus, making them quite opinionated. Consequently, this has made the older women to feel that their opinion and guidance will not be adhered to or even considered if they do take on a mentorship role. However, it is important to know that younger women nowadays are eagerly seeking guidance and are also in need of it. So, an older woman who might have the characteristics mentioned above and feels comfortable and led to mentor younger women, shouldn't let fear of failure overtake her. I'd suggest she steps out in faith by reaching out to the younger women in her church community.

So, the question is, what does an effective mentoring relationship look like?

Here are a few qualities of an effective mentoring relationship.

1. Accessibility

It is important that this older woman is accessible. It's vital that she has time, etc. She does not have to be a Bible scholar to mentor another woman. Nonetheless, she should love the God of the Bible and want to abide by His Word. It is crucial that she also has an active love relationship with Jesus.

Being available with timely and godly advice can make the difference for an individual who is without an anchor. It is an essential necessity for younger women to have the experience, fortitude and sample of older women. It is true that there are many other people to give advice and guidance. Additionally, while prayer is wise when seeking discernment in how much mentoring one should do, how many hours to commit, etc., the basic idea of "Do I become a mentor?" is clearly commanded in scripture. She should be obedient, and available.

2. Focus

It is important that this older woman is focussed and that this relationship has a goal to make the most of the younger woman's time with her. Questions such as: 'What is this younger woman seeking from a relationship with me?' should be asked. It could be that she is seeking an enhanced understanding of the Bible? It could also be that she needs guidance as she starts a new Christian business or even as she ventures into that which God has for her. She might just need encouragement from someone a few steps ahead of her, to aid when taking a leap of faith in obedience to Jesus. On the other hand, what if she really just wants a prayer partner, someone who will help her establish a better devotional life? The older woman should not feel compelled to run out and buy a Bible study plan but rather pray with her. Moreover, this young woman might just need nurturing help because she didn't grow up in a Christian home and has no model to follow. If this older woman has older children, she may be the perfect match for her. It is important that this older woman understands that mentoring a younger woman is not always through Bible study.

3. Innovation

It's important that this older woman is able to change things up and think outside the box to make their relationship fun and interesting. It is important that this older woman does not to make meetings uninteresting and mind-numbing. It is important that you meet regularly. Making scheduled time and days of meeting to suit both parties and there is always room for variation. They can go out for coffee, meet for breakfast, and have afternoon tea as long as it's a time and place that meets the needs of both parties. The older woman can try to schedule it in activities which they can share – walking, running, cooking, and hiking. It all depends on their personalities and the focus of their relationship. But it's important that relationship is built on a not so formal foundation. Christian mentoring isn't about being intensely spiritual all the time, it's about building relationships.

4. Attentiveness

When this older woman has managed to get together with this new friend, it is important that she listens and let the younger woman open up. Sometimes this is where the older woman misses the mark. They tend to come across as impulsive because they are not listening and feel compelled to dole out advice for every topic she might raise. It is important that this older woman waits until she asks for her thoughts before offering them. It is so crucial that this older woman is trust worthy. Many young women have had their trust broken at different times and it will be of no benefit to her if this older woman has a loose tongue. The person she mentors must be able to trust her implicitly and know that nothing they tell her will ever be taken any further. It is a completely sacred relationship. This is the beauty of it as it encourages vulnerability and this can bring healing to the young woman's heart if this older woman is Godly and wise!

5. Unpretentiousness

One thing that often scares younger women away is when they feel like the older women will not be able to understand or that they cannot relate. When it is time to do the talking, it's vital that this older woman remembers that honesty makes her vulnerable. She is to remember that we were all sinners saved by grace, continuing to be transformed into the image of Christ; none of us is a finished product yet! Therefore, she should not be afraid of being genuine, through revealing her weakness and how she's overcome the ones she has. Of course there's a level of revelation that should take place depending on the focus and type of relationship it is. The older woman should be happy to share her weaknesses when asked but should use discretion. As I said earlier, it depends on the focus of the relationship and the type.

6. Model

This older woman should be a role model. The reason why this young woman may have come to her was because she felt she could do the job. So, it's important that you keep being the role model that she needs by the empowerment of the Holy Spirit. There is a phrase, "Do as I say, not as I do," which is as dishonourable in mentoring as it is in parenting. Older women mentors must show their trustworthiness, demonstrate their love for God, and actually pray when they say they will. We all are very guilty of this when we say we'll pray but we don't. Words alone are empty. The older woman should be like Paul, who encouraged the Corinthian church to do as he did: **"Follow my example, as I**

follow the example of Christ. I praise you for re-membering me in everything and for holding to the teachings, just as I passed them on to you" (1 Corinthians 11:1-2). She should be an example not just by words but by deeds. Most people nowadays are broken because of people who have failed them especially when they saw this person as a role model.

7. Instructing/Teaching

Some mentoring relationships require an older woman to teach the younger woman she is men-toring. Sometimes these teachings can take place in the form of a bible study on various topics or a specific topic. These topics can range from busi-ness, to inferiority complex, or even healthy living. Most times these teaching can be in a formal setting such as meeting at a local church or as informal as a breakfast café. The older woman can also teach from life experiences and also things that she has learned from those above her. It is pivotal that this older woman makes sure that the teaching is tailored to her mentee's need so that the young woman can get as much understanding and knowledge as she needs. It's also important that as this older woman teaches, she allows the younger woman to practice what she has been taught. This will help her know that the teaching is being beneficial to the younger woman. It's important that she does not shut down the younger woman when she raises an opinion that's contrary to hers. If she does that it's manipulation and it's not healthy to their relationship. The differences in opinions should be discussed with an end goal to reach a common ground based on the scriptures.

To conclude, things will look different in each relationship, but mentors must find ways to encourage and develop godliness in the younger women. Whatever purpose brought them together, it's important that she challenges her in that area of life, encouraging her to step out in faith and wisdom, gleaned from the older woman and others, also believing the Lord for everything.

CHERUB
Young Woman

Chapter 8

Young Woman

What does it mean to be a young Christian girl? There's no way we can understand what it means to be a young CHRISTIAN girl, without understanding what it means to be a young girl. A young girl is a female child who is not yet able to make decisions onher own by law or morally. A young girl is still under the covering of an adult figure, be it in a family structure, by law via fostering or guardianship, she is also not recognised as an adult by law and in some cases morally. A young girl goes through many stages in her life that can be said to be the factors that make up who she will be as an adult. Therefore what demarcates the young 'Christian' girl from the regular young girl? It's something called choice. Even if a female child has been raised in a Christian home it does not solidify her being a Christian. Yes of course it introduces her to the faith but she has to make a choice to trust the Lord with all her heart and lean not on her own understanding and He shall direct her path (Proverbs 3:5).

A young Christian girl upholds Christ and godly values in the time of self-discovery. In this stage of her life, she is only just beginning to understand the type of person she is. She is yet to have the advantage of many life experiences so, she is quite naïve to what life has in store for her. This therefore means that she can become quite frightened which might lead her to start doing things that she knows aren't good for her as she is stepping into what I call the 'unknown'. At this stage, it is vital that she has a very deep reverence for God's word and His commands. Without that, she would not be able to distinguish between the voice of God and her voice. The bible says the fear of the Lord is the beginning of wisdom, (Proverbs 9:10). What does it mean to fear the Lord? When she fears the Lord, she is in absolute devotion to his will and purposes; she dies to her flesh by letting go of her personal desires and by submitting to the spirit of God. For this to happen she needs to accept that she needs the help of God via his Holy Spirit through His Son Jesus Christ.

As a young girl she might feel as though she has made many mistakes and this might make her feel unworthy of the teaching and guidance of the Holy Spirit. However, God sent His son to die on the cross for her that she may be set free from sin and that she might have everlasting life in His presence

(John 3:16). Nevertheless, she needs to understand that God frees us from the judgement of sin but not from the consequences. This means that the actions she takes or the choices she makes as a young Christian woman could shape the rest of her life. It is important that she makes the most godly decision possible by seeking wise counsel as in there is safety. (Proverbs 11:, 24:6, 15:22). A young Christian girl must be fierce in her pursuit of God. She must understand that she is evolving into that which God wants her to be and that it is best for her to know her God in the days of her youth.

Ecclesiastes 12:1 (New International Version)
Remember your Creator in the days of your youth, before the days of trouble come and the years approach when you will say, "I find no pleasure in them"

This scripture is so key to every young Christian girl. She does not want to get to the prime of her youth or her ripe age and then start to recount the mistakes she made and how things could have been better if she had done this and that. She needs to lay hold of God as soon as she comes into the reality that she can choose God for herself. It is understood that not all young girls grow in Christian homes where they are exposed to God from a very tender age. However, one beautiful thing about that is that when this young girl then chooses to come to the realisation of the Lamb of God Jesus, she should choose Him quick and fast.

A Y.C.G should not forget God and just think that because she recited the Lord's prayer she can do as she pleases afterwards because she is now saved, no. That scripture is telling her to recognise her God in the time when all her desires suddenly become gratified, as she seeks pleasure and passions. The root word for remember in that scripture is to 'properly mark (so as to be recognised)' This means this young Christian girl needs to understand the need to properly recognise the superiority of God in her life and His very close presence.

A YCG is not afraid of the future because she understands Jeremiah 29: 11.

Jeremiah 29:11 (New International Version)
11 For I know the plans I have for you," declares the Lord, "plans to prosper you and not to harm you, plans to give you hope and a future.

She needs to be able to trust the Lord because as she grows, she is bound to go through many trials and tribulations and a good foundation in God is what keeps her in perfect peace through it. A Y.C.G is respectful to God and his authorities over her. She is willing to learn from people but also willing to allow the Holy Spirit to teach her on how to discern what to take on board and what to dismiss. A Y.C.G allows the Holy Spirit to teach her how to guard her heart from unnecessary things that could make her compromise her values. 'The heart is the seat of values and convictions' Apostle Elijah Chanak.

Chapter 9

How can she develop self-worth?

*T*here are many teachings surrounding this particular topic and also many suggestions on how low self-esteem can be overcome. Even in the world, there are many teachings and guides on how to develop confidence and self-worth, etc. Many times we are tempted to absolutely love and adore ourselves which of course is not bad in itself. It is important, however to note that any self-worth found outside of Christ is artificial. When you look at self-worth through the lenses of Jesus the Christ, we will see it in a completely different light.

Scripture says that were created in the image and in the likeness of God (Genesis 1:27). This therefore means that we are mirror reflections of God. Therefore, when the mirror moves there is no reflection. The mirror is bare and the subject of reflection sees no reflection. This is what happened when Adam stepped outside of the presence of God this was evident when they hid as they heard God walk in the cool of the day!

What is self-worth? The common definition is the sense of one's own value or worth as a person. Nonetheless, that is in the eyes of the world. A young Christian woman might be thinking 'but, that definition makes a lot of sense'. However, if she does not understand it biblically, she would miss the mark. First, she has to understand that she has no worth outside of Christ. Let's break this down. In God all things were created and scripture says in John 1:1 that in the beginning was the word and the word was with God, and the word was God. As we know, Christ is the Word of God made manifest in flesh. The word there is in capital W, this denotes that it is Jesus Christ. Jesus the Christ is the personal wisdom and power in union with God. It can be understood as Him being God's minister in creation and administration of the universe. He is the root of all life. So Jesus is not an instant idea that God had, He is the manifold wisdom of God in human flesh. How generous is our God! Consequently, a YCW outside of the knowledge of Christ, not just head knowledge but heart transforming knowledge, is bound to go through the identity crisis palaver.

Before she can even understand her worth as a young woman, she has to understand her worth as a Christian; that she was bought with a price. God wanted to reconcile with us after the fall of man in Genesis, that he sent His son to die for us and take us back from the hands of the enemy.

A young christian wowan(YCW) needs to understand that Christ has paid her bride price; she must now accept Him and marry him. For Him to come into human form and be so lowly just for her, shows her how much she is worth in His eyes. Most times, the issue of self-worth is over-looked in the Christian community. Some YCW have been taught to focus on being 'good girls' so that they can get 'good husbands' to marry. Yet, the women in the churches have failed to teach them that they need to be women of virtue not just to get 'good husbands' but to fulfil purpose in Christ alongside the godly husband that God gives to them. They are princesses in the eyes of God and nothing can separate them from His love. Unfortunately, society and media has outlined who they are supposed to be; therefore the standards of the world are now what they live by. They have not been taught or maybe have forgotten that they ought to have dominion in all spheres of their lives. The YCW is meant to be the standard that other young women in the world look to imitate. She should carry herself with grace, be reverent in all behaviour. However, in most cases it is not her fault that she does not know these things. These young women aren't usually taught these things at home most especially when they have unbelieving parents. This now means that there are very few examples around.

I understand that they are many things that a YCW might have gone through, which probably no one knows about because she is sacred and ashamed to let any ear hear. Nevertheless, God is on her side. I know that is hard to believe because she might ask herself 'how can I grow up around Christians, attend church but none could see what was going on?'

You see, there are things that God lets her go through as a Christian child and young woman, so that she can defeat the enemy by the word of her testimony (Revelation 12:11).

God lets the enemy deal with her so that she can see the need for him. Her testimony will cause Him to be lifted up, so that he draws others unto Him. The society we live in is not a suitable place to raise a young Christian woman. We have different ideologies and definitions of self-worth. Young Christian women are finding worth in what the world defines as worth. Being able to attract the most handsome boys/men is seen as having worth by some folks. Being able to 'show off what your momma gave to you', having multiple boyfriends, and being popular is mis-read as a marker of self-worth. She has been taught that self-worth is when she feels appreciated because a male buys her chocolate, flowers and takes her on expensive shopping trips. She has been taught that self-worth is when she has premarital sex so that she is able to 'keep her man'. She has been taught that self-worth is when she feels valued by the grades she gets at her educational institutions, because she is able to go into the world to get a 'good job' and be 'Miss Independent'.

However she's blind to the fact that she is worth much more than she can ever imagine. The Lord says that she is fearfully and wonderfully created.

When she starts to believe this, there will be an outward manifestation. What she does not grasp is that God took his time to create her; He took his time to think of her physical features which she has failed to embrace even though they are unique to her. He took time to construct that very nose or legs she does not like, she needs to be appreciative of what she has. The Lord delights in looking at her and He finds pleasure in loving her.

Self-worth is very important because it opens her eyes so that she is able to walk confidently in the Lord. It is important that she knows that she means so much to the Lord.

Self-worth stems from a place of an intimate relationship with the Lord. He longs to have an intimate relationship with her; He wants to get to know her. Yes, He knows all about her already and He most definitely knows all the contents of her heart. However, the main reason why He wants to have an intimate relationship with her is so that He can pour out the contents of His heart out to her, and share His secrets with her. He wants her to know the contents of His heart. Scripture says that the secrets of the Lord are with those that reverence Him (Psalm 25:14). He longs for her to know His purpose for her. Through an intimate relationship with the Lord, she will find out that she is worth more than she thinks. She is priceless, He died for HER! Nothing can beat that, nothing! Yahweh wants to lavish her with love. She needs to allow Him, it is only in Him that she will be able to find love, worth and purpose.

Chapter 10

What is purpose?

For a YCW, walking the way God wants her to means that she is walking according to his plans and purposes for her life. It is vital that she does this so that she does not live an aimless and unfulfilled life. It is essential that she knows how treasurable she is and how much Abba loves her. He sent His only son to die for her sins, so that she might also appear blameless before God in fellowship and reconciliation with Him. He has given life and life more abundantly to those who will receive it.

For a YCW to understand who she is, she'll need to understand why she was created and, to understand why she was created, she has to go back to her creator. It makes more sense to understand who she is and then why she was created. Doing it the other way round is like trying to find a solution to an unidentified problem. It is just like what every Christian should do; know their identity as sons/daughters of God when they surrender their lives to Him and then through that, they can find out their purpose in Him. They find out their function and His calling over their lives, be it to the church or the market place (the world). However, there still needs to be a purpose for something and through its purpose and characteristics it is then given an identity. Instances abound in the bible to show that when a child will be named, they are usually named after their purpose or after a circumstance. For example Jacob and Esau, they were given those names because they were already fighting from the womb. Rebekah had inquired of the Lord and found out their purpose. Also Benjamin who was formerly Benoni was named by his mother, Rachel, as the son of her sorrow. She had waited for him for many years after the birth of her first son, Joseph. Also his birth was hard on her and she passed on after having him. His name was however changed to Benjamin which means 'son of my right hand'. The right hand represents strength and when his father was blessing all his children in prophecy he said Benjamin will be a ravenous wolf, a warrior almost.

Furthermore, in Genesis 1:5, God created light and then called it day and the darkness he called night. See the keyword there 'called'. He called after he had given it purpose. We also see this pattern throughout Genesis. As God created, He approved; meaning he gave identity. Therefore, to understand who she is, a YCW has to go back to God and ask Him why he created her. She can't fulfil purpose if she does not understand and walk in it.

Purpose is not just a slogan to be put across the forehead. It is something that we were born for. A young Christian woman's primary purpose is to love and worship Jesus. She is to make Him famous and to be a fisher of men for the Kingdom of God. However each of us have different ways in which we function in this God given commission to believers. This is where a young woman needs to ask God where she is placed specifically in the body of Christ. We all know that every part of the body has its functions and they all do what they need to do so that the individual is effective. We also know that when a part of the body is sick, the rest of the body fights their hardest to keep it alive or heal it. This is how a young Christian woman should see purpose. It is important though that she first pursues God not just for purpose but for intimacy. The bible says knowledge puffs up (1 Corinthians 8:1). It is pivotal that intimacy with God is her first pursuit after which all will be added (Matthew 6:33). Purpose naturally flows from intimacy.

A young Christian woman should, however, not be ignorant of the things God calls her to do.

It does not always have to start big. Most times it can start as small as leading bible study in her home with her siblings. It can also be caring for an elderly neighbour in the hope of sharing the Gospel of Jesus Christ with them. It is important that she obeys in the little instructions she might get from God. As she obeys, God begins to give her more understanding and possibly lead her unto greater things. She will also show the Lord that she can be faithful in the little things (Luke 16:10).

The most important thing is that she will know as she follows on to know the Lord and He will go forth and come to her like rain (Hosea 6:3).

Then we shall know, if we follow on to know the Lord: his going forth is prepared as the morning: and he shall come unto us as the rain, as the latter and former unto the earth

This means that she is assured that she will know the Lord if she follows on to know because in Christ He promises that she should have that inward knowledge of Him, which is ever growing, because of grace through which it is given. It continues to grow, it is an unsearchable depth. As a result He will come to her as morning full of joy and comfort. This is to say, her constant pursuit will cause God to come to her as she longs for morning. He will then come to her as rain as the former and latter..

Isn't God beautiful?

PRIME
Nearly there

Introduction

*T*here are many things we need to consider when we look into the prime of our youth. It is important for a young woman to be able to mature and adapt to the fact that she is now an adult and would have to make decisions that can build her or ruin her. The prime is between the ages of 18 until 22 (this is not completely accurate). This is because the young woman is at a time where she might have stopped puberty.

At this stage a young woman is going through many transitions, this is when she leaves the nest and in some cases moves out or goes off to university. She has cultivated a sense of individuality and now she has the opportunity to nurture it. This young woman will also have developed solid friendships or might be looking to develop some. She is quite clear on what her desires and her preferences are. She is more careful in her approach to developing relationships and is less carefree as she might have been in her younger days. It is vital that in this stage of her life this young woman is surrounded by supportive friends and family, as during this prime time of her life, she's prone to making quite a lot of mistakes and will need support to overcome the consequences.

As a Christian young woman it is important that she seeks God like never before. She is to make sure that she is constantly at the feet of Jesus as He will need to guide her through these different stages of self-discovery.

So sit back as we will be discussing the different things that might affect a young Christian woman as she grows through this stage of her life. These issues can also be applicable to even the younger and older women.

Chapter 11

Mind

There's no way we can understand mind-sets and how they are formed without first understanding the role of the mind. A mind-set is the fruit of the mind and it's interaction with experiences, background and upbringing. So that means we have different mind-sets for different things.

So we will be discussing what the mind is, its importance, the things that affect the mind, what type of mind a young Christian woman should have, how to cultivate this mind, how mind-sets are formed and what mind-set is expected of a young Christian woman?

When we look at the mind, there are many definitions that surround this word and quite a number of different perspectives. I'd like to first give the Oxford dictionary definition which is the 'element of a person that enables them to be aware of the world and their experiences, to think, and to feel; the faculty of consciousness and thought.' This therefore means that the mind is where most of us determine what our course of action will be after certain thoughts or experiences. Therefore, it is important that the mind is in a stable place where it is able to judge thoughts and experiences, before the individual takes the appropriate course of action. When studying the mind as a young Christian woman it is important that you know what influences the mind and also how to overcome negative influences on the mind. Let me emphasise here that the mind is also very important as it helps with the acknowledgement of our uniqueness and understanding of God. The human mind however is flawed. It is quite egocentric and this is against the ways of God. The human mind can be fed negatively by the flesh. The flesh is a hard layer between the spirit and the soul. The flesh is the foundation that coated the human spirit when man fell in the garden of Eden. It is this same flesh that brings resistance to the Holy Spirit of God. All was because man became sin-conscious (2 Corinthians 4:1-6). Ever since the flesh coated the human spirit (spiritual death) and as a result resisted God, the mind of man has been flawed and distorted, living outside the mind of God, hence the many atrocities committed by mankind to mankind.

Now that we understand that the mind is faulty due to its dwelling outside of God, we can understand why we are prone to producing bad fruits (Luke 6:43). The human mind outside of God will cause us to do things that are out of His will for us. The reason why our minds, outside of God, cause us to produce bad fruit is because we have hardened hearts. We are not able to perceive God; neither are we able to discern His will for us.

When a young woman repents and believes the gospel, she is given a new heart. However, she needs to make sure that she renews her mind. The scripture in Romans 12:2 says that we should not be conformed to this world, but be transformed by the renewing of our mind. As I had explained earlier the mind needs to have some sort of interaction with experiences, background and upbringing for it to produce a mind-set. This is why the mind needs to be renewed, so that when it interacts with experiences, background and upbringing it can then produce fruits that prove what the good, acceptable and perfect will of God is. Renew means to restore to a former state. In that scripture (Romans 12:2), renewing is a feminine noun word, and it is also a verb that suggests continuity. This therefore means that to renew is to cause a conscious continuous act of bringing the word of God in contact with the mind. This causes it to be sanctified and cleansed by the washing of water by the word, thus resulting in the continuous production of good fruit.

The mind is very important to the everyday living of a human being. It helps them reason and it's unique to them. As a young Christian woman, your mind is highly important to the excellency of your walk with God and knowledge of Christ. A man called Pastor T. Jay once said that the excellency of the knowledge of Jesus is in stages. This therefore means that maturity is in stages. So, if a young Christian woman's mind is maladjusted, she might just miss the excellency of the knowledge of Christ. She needs to understand that her mind needs to be washed by the word regularly so that she might conduct herself well and that she is also able to be effective here on earth with everything God has placed in her. If her mind is not being renewed she might make grievous mistakes even though it was out of a pure heart. A stagnant mind in the things of God can also put a cap on her spirit man because there will be constant conflict and if care is not taken it might result in a slumbering spirit.

There are many things that affect the mind but I believe the most prominent ones are upbringing and life experiences. We understand that everything outside of God is a lie as God is truth. Therefore, if a young woman was not brought up in the ways and fear of the Lord as Proverbs 22:6 and Ephesians 6:4 commands, she will not be able to continue with the Lord. The thing with most young 'Christian' women is that they have been brought up in religion and have never had the opportunity to build relationships with God. They were presented with a flawed image of the gospel. Well this applies to women who were born into Christian homes. The ones who were not also didn't get an opportunity to know the Lord so therefore, they have grown up with ideologies that are contrary to scripture. Their minds are conformed to the ways of this world and their course of action, based on their experiences, is fashioned according to the system of the world.

Now what type of mind is expected of a young Christian woman? As I was about to write this answer, I got stuck and asked the Lord to remind me and He said 'hope', which makes perfect sense! Why? As YCW we are expected to have a common ground when it comes to the mind. One thing the Holy Spirit dropped in my heart was that we are meant to have a common mind of hope. This way, when our mind comes in contact with experiences, trials and tribulations, our character is matured and our faith is approved because we have acted as a result of the simplicity, wisdom and humility found in hope.

This leads us to the question: 'what is hope'? We know that Christ in us is our hope of glory (Colossians 1:27). According to the Oxford Dictionary, hope is the feeling that what is wanted can be had or that events will turn out for the best. Now as I wrote this, I asked the Holy Spirit what He meant by this. Then He made me to understand that as YCW, since Christ is in us we have hope for glory. That is to say that our minds are meant to be fixed to count it all joy when we fall into trials and tribulations (James 1:2). Let me break this down a bit.

James 1 New International Version (NIV)

1 James, a bondservant of God and of the Lord Jesus Christ, to the twelve tribes which are scattered abroad: Greetings. 2 My brethren, count it all joy when you fall into various trials,

In the first verse we see here that James is described as a bond servant, that means he was one who gave himself up to another's will, that is the will of God. His service is used by Christ in extending and advancing his cause among men. This means that what he will be saying next will definitely be validated by the spirit of God since scripture is God breathed. So in verse two we see that it says 'count it all joy' the root word there is 'ago' and it means to 'lay hold of and this way by doing so brings to a place of destination'. The word trial is 'peircismo' and it means experiments and experiment is the testing of a principle. The principle being our faith and it also means the act or operation of discovering something unknown. So in other words that verse is saying 'My brethren lay hold of all joy when you fall into diverse experiments because it is the testing of your faith to discover something unknown. This is proven by the scripture in Hebrews 11:1

Now faith is the assurance of things hoped for, the conviction of things not seen.

So the mind set of hope is laying hold of joy knowing that the end will be good! Jeremiah 29:11:

11 For I know the plans I have for you," declares the Lord, "plans to prosper you and not to harm you, plans to give you hope and a future

Again, this scripture in Jeremiah 29:11 encourages us to lay hold of this joy to help us be hopeful of this mysterious expected end!

The verse 3- 4 of James 1 goes like this:

3 knowing that the testing of your faith produces patience. 4 But let patience have its perfect work, that you may be perfect and complete, lacking nothing.

This shows that when we lay hold of joy in our trial we will then have the testing of our faith produce patience in us. The word 'but' in this context is an adversative conjunction and it is expressing contrariety. This suggests that even after going through the trials, we may not have faith and patience do that which we need to do. The phrase 'perfect work', suggests that change will have taken place, but it won't mature! "Patience is an intense active energy not a mere passive endurance" – McLaren. Patience is the FULL consent of a yielding will, that is to say patience is the conversion of our souls during sanctification. It takes patience to go from Justification (point of acceptance and initiation), Sanctification (Point of pruning and the growth, renewing of the mind, submission of the will, sturdiness of emotions and change of heart) and Glorification (Point of being changed from mortals to immortals and re-union with Jesus our bridegroom).

So when we come into the knowledge of Christ, we are expected to have a mind of hope. This is what Christ had. He took a huge step by dying for us. He had hope that His death will turn out for the best and that He will have a bride at the end of it all. Even now He still has hope because His bride is still being formed and He keeps interceding for her daily. As we know, we are meant to imitate Christ. This means that we are encouraged to hope until the end. When our mind is like the mind of Christ, we are able to interact better with experiences, trials and tribulations; therefore producing good fruit!

Chapter 12

Desires

When desires are brought up, most people begin to think negatively. In fact as we know desires go both ways. As a matter of fact the bible encourages having desires. It makes it clear that God is willing to give us our hearts desires according to His will, when we delight in Him. This is an amazing thing that most of us YCW are not able to fully comprehend. It sounds so easy and calm but there is a lot more to making sure that we fine tune our desires to the frequency of the will of God. This requires a lot from us, the only way it can be fully formed in us is if we pursue intimacy with the Jesus the Christ.

Permit me to quickly delve into intimacy. Intimacy is communion with God. It is being able to have a transparent love type of fellowship with God. Intimacy is not a thing of just words; it is validated by a faithful and pliable heart coupled with actions of love and reverence. Once upon a time, I gave a little exhortation at a fellowship on the difference between relationship and intimacy.

It is possible to have a relationship and not have intimacy. When I looked at what relationship means it said 'A state of being connected by BLOOD or MARRIAGE'. Now I hear many people say that they have a relationship with God and that is very true, every believer has a relationship with God. Once you believe in His Son Jesus the Christ and you turn away from your sins you are therefore initiated by His blood into a covenant relationship with the God-head. When Jesus justified us with His blood, that automatically positioned us for a relationship with Him.

Now when you look at relationship, you see that

there are two words that have been joined together to make one. Relation being the first and it means 'connection' and ship being the other and it means 'mode of transportation'. Furthermore, when we see that word, it represents our salvation, so that means it's the fact that we have salvation, it is the carrier of our connection/affiliation with God. Consequently, intimacy is then built on this automatic relationship by grace that we have with God.

Now there are many reasons why people backslide and one of the main reasons is as a result of having a stale relationship. Scripture says that any branch that does not bear fruit is cut off. So it's not that God hates a YCW when she backslides, it's just a principle that has to take place because it's been spoken and written. When a relationship is stale, it means it is not thriving, flourishing, growing etc. Therefore intimacy will be absent in a stale relationship.

The difference between an average relationship and thriving relationship is working out. To work out is to perform, or to render one fit for a thing. Now this is where most of us get it mixed up. Some people have the idea that once I give my life to Jesus, all I have to do is attend church, have my early morning devotion and go about my day. Some others think working out their relationship is doing their daily devotions, going to church regularly, having fellowship with the saints, serving at church and they're cool. Both ideologies are wrong when the word is not made flesh and when you don't encounter Jesus every day. Now I am not talking about daily angelic visitations which are AWESOME if you get those. I am talking about letting God become your reality, when you no longer have an opinion.

Most times we do these things that are awesome but they are usually done out of a heart that has not surrendered to the divine working of the Holy-Spirit. That's why most saints get tired and weary; they usually do not experience God in their communion with Him. They almost form this falsehood of intimacy as the Israelites did. Going to their place of worship, dropping their sacrifice and forgetting their God once they stepped out of that place. Therefore, it is important that an atmosphere (mind, spirit and soul) is cultivated to maintain constant fellowship with God. This can only be done when there is true surrender to the ways and the will of God. It is when the YCW needs to make a conscious decision daily to live out the word she not only reads but hears!

When a YCW walks with God and develops a thriving relationship with Him, her desires are bound to be fine-tuned because she has delighted herself in Him.

So, what does it mean to 'delight thyself also in the Lord'? When we look into this scripture Psalms 37:4 we see that it is a continuation of something that had been said before due to the word 'also'. The verse prior to that verse begins with "trust in the Lord". Therefore from understanding, the Holy Spirit has made me realise that it is impossible to delight in someone that you do not trust. When we look at the Hebrew meaning of delight it means, to be soft or pliable. Therefore we see that to delight in the Lord means being pliable before him and being able to adjust readily to change instead of being rigid. It also means yielding, being easily influenced. When a YCW also has these qualities in God, he then says he will give her the desires of her heart. But there's a catch, her desires are out of the window when she is easily influenced or yielded. She is prone to latching onto the desires of the person she is being influenced by. So what that scripture is saying is that, her desires will automatically change when she yields herself to God. Her desires will be refined and now, it'll no longer be that she desires this and that, but it will be a cry of 'let thy will be done oh Lord!'

There are many things that a YCW will desire as she grows in biblical womanhood, but here are a few.

- To find her specific place in the body of Christ
- To have lasting friendships
- To have an identity of her own
- To have companionship

To find their place in the body of Christ; this is one thing that most people and not just young Christian women desire. It's a desire that God has placed in the heart of his people so that they might function effectively. This is a legitimate desire and one that will bring her a great deal of fulfilment. Abba wants each and every one of us to feel valuable and useful. He desires that we find the place that he has called us to be. A young woman should not hesitate to ask God to show her the path to the fulfilment of Her God-ordained purpose. The thing is, she might have already started to do things that can indicate her purpose and she might not know it. She needs to ask God to enlighten her. Hear His word: **I will instruct you and teach thee in the way which you shall go: I will guide you with my eye** (Psalms 32:8)

She also needs to seek wise counsel, scripture says in the multitude of counsel there is safety (Proverbs 15:22). One thing one of my brothers in Christ said to me was that I should learn to fine tune my thoughts so that I can hear God's still small voice. This is so crucial. Fine tuning your thoughts means seating at the feet of Jesus. One thing that helps me make this a reality is literally picturing myself sitting in front of beautiful glowing bronze feet (Revelation 1:15)

His feet were like bronze glowing in a furnace, and his voice was like the sound of rushing waters.

I have this picture in my mind all day and I just speak to Jesus, pray and worship as I go through the day. When my thoughts are about to drift, I just whisper to Jesus to help me.

The desire to find her specific place in the body of Christ should however not overwhelm and sidetrack seeking first the kingdom of God and His righteousness.

Having Lasting Friendships

Having lasting friendships is one things everyone longs for, so a young woman needs to seek the Lord on how to create friendships and also which to keep and which to bring to a close. Her friends are a huge influence on her so the intervention of the Lord is required. The next two chapters will be dealing with this in depth.

To have an identity of her own

Many people want to have that one thing that defines them and makes them who they are. It is a good desire and one that should not be neglected. But a young woman needs to know that it is dangerous that, in her aim to be unique and different, she misses what God has for her and portrays God wrongly to others. Many women now are doing so many things to 'do YOU' not knowing that in doing that, they are promoting their flesh and the wicked desire of their heart. It's important that a young woman checks the motive behind the things she does or says. A young woman's identity stems from her mind and her will. Her mind is usually what determines whether or not she understands her identity as a member of the body of Christ. This can only take place if she renews her mind. She should also submit her will to God so that His will for her and her identity in Him can flourish.

To have companionship

This one is HUGE amongst our young women. These days, it is becoming increasingly popular that our young women are seeking out companions in the wrong places. The body of Christ is one agent that fuels this ever growing desire. It is true that this desire is not bad. However, it can quickly become sour when it is not fulfilled at the desired time for the person involved. Believers on social media have now made it seem like it is such a necessity to frequently post updates about their partners and their relationships. I believe it is quite wicked and insensitive to continually post about the joys of a relationship and not the let-downs, the beautiful flowers and not the heated arguments; as this generation is, we take these things at face-value and base our understanding of companionship on what our celebrity-like Christians post.

Social media is only but a glimpse and humans being humans will only share what they want you to see. This is why a young woman should look to Jesus as the only standard of what companionship should look like.

Many times we as believers complain about attacks from people and people talking about us and the things we do. However we tend to forget that sometimes we are the architects of our own destruction/predicaments. We put ourselves out there without the use of wisdom but then fuss at people when they attack us or speak against that which we do. The members of the younger generation are not skilful at the internalisation of things until they become ripe. An African proverb says "the kolanut that hides itself, is the one that ripens". We complain and say "I am human like you" when we fall short of the pedestal we place ourselves on.

Ponder!

Chapter 13

Modesty

What is modesty? Most times when a young Christian woman hears modesty, the first thing that she thinks of is how well covered she is by her clothes and how appropriate she seems to the human eye. However, I would like to say that modesty first begins in the mind. This is a notion that most people might object to discussing because it might come off as quite unusual. If I were to define modesty, I would define it as a respectable manner of adorning one's body and carrying oneself, born out of a freedom from a worldly definition of beauty and worth, and encouraged by a disgust to sin and a desire to pull devotion to God. According to the dictionary, modesty is the quality of being modest; freedom from vanity, boastfulness.

Therefore, the most basic definition of modesty is being free from ostentation or showy extravagance.

As earlier stated, modesty first begins in the mind. A YCW's thoughts stem from her mind and her mind is usually the birthing place of her behaviours. I will go into that later on. Firstly, scripture says that she should have the mind that was also in Christ (Philippians 2:5). It is so crucial that she has this because without the mind of Christ it is impossible to have His attributes and have His conduct. She should be an imitator of Christ even in her thoughts.

The character of modesty

The Inner Character of Modesty: Holiness of Mind. (1 Peter 1:13-16 NIV)

13 Therefore, with minds that are alert and fully sober, set your hope on the grace to be brought to you when Jesus Christ is revealed at his coming. 14 As obedient children, do not con-

form to the evil desires you had when you lived in ignorance. 15 But just as he who called you is holy, so be holy in all you do; 16 for it is written: "Be holy, because I am holy."

The ordering is not of dress and demeanour only, but of the inner life expressing itself outwardly. Sobriety (sober) means to be in moderation, soundness of mind and sound judgment. It is used in the sense of being free from intoxicants of worldly values and lusts (1Pet 3:2-4). It also means conduct that is restrained, and is not ostentatious or showy (1 Tim 2:9). It is consistent with the profession of godliness (1 Tim 2:10).

To be modest in thought is to be rid of pride. There's no way a YCW can be modest in her mind and her thoughts when they are high and lofty. The bible says that God resists the prideful (James 4:6). He is not their friend and He wants no communion with them. Pride stems from the Sin Nature.

In fact, it's the first born of the Sin Nature (Hebrew: Harmatia). Due to her sin nature she might believe she is above the governance and sovereignty of God. This is pride.

It is impossible to please God when her thoughts concerning Him, others and herself are impure, high and lofty and even insecure. It is so important to make sure that there is a lack of vanity in how she thinks of herself. No one has attained, even Apostle Paul agreed that he had not yet attained (Philippians 3:12). She should not think lowly of others (Romans 12:16). She should also think well of herself (Song of Solomon 4:7) in the sense of sober judgement and according to the grace God has assigned to her as an individual in Christ (Romans 12:3).

Scripture commands that she renews her mind as part of her working out her salvation with fear and trembling (Romans 12:2). It is pivotal that she understands that without this she will not be able to discern the will of God. This therefore means that she is unable to grow in fulfilling the reason for which she was created; the purpose and pleasure of God. A heart of modesty is motivated by a love for one's fellow human.

Modesty in behaviour

Modesty is about behaviour and attitude, not just clothing. To be modest in behaviour is to be modest in speech, relationships and, last but not the least, character. It is vital that as a YCW she is modest in the way she speaks to and about others; careful about the words that proceed from her mouth. It is crucial for every Christian to be Modest in Behaviour, 1 Pet 2:11-12 (virtuous).

Modesty also shows her sensitivity to sin which will in turn affect her behaviour. 1 Timothy 2:9, Paul says a woman's apparel should be worn with "modesty." Other translations opt for the word "decency." The King James Version translates this as "shamefacedness," which gets more to the heart of the word. I also believe that this scripture applies to both men and women in this day and age. Both genders dress very immodestly.

It is talking about a demeanour of reverence, showing respect to oneself and a regard for others. It even carries the connotation of "bashful." Connected to the term "shame," the word implies the idea of grief over sin that is in the world—we should be so sensitive to sin, knowing that sin is offensive to God, that we would never come close to trying to provoke it in others thoughts, their character and their speech etc.

A young woman should seek to dress her life in works that do well to others, marked with godly love. This means modesty is not simply about what she wears, but how she acts, how she communicates, and how she relates to others. When Paul says that women should wear "respectable apparel," the term "apparel" is probably translated too narrowly: it is a term that encompasses not just clothing, but one's whole demeanour, attitude, and actions. Ultimately, what should adorn a woman is not just clothing but "good works." As Christians, we are being remade by God for good works (Ephesians 2:10). Christ died so that we might be zealous for good works (Titus 2:14).

As a YCW, it is essential that she learns how to speak in a respectful way to others. It is crucial that she is modest in the way she says things to people. Her words should be seasoned with grace and salt (Colossians 2:6); it should be soothing to the soul (proverbs 16:24). This is all part of being modest in our behaviour.

I'll quickly summarise in my own words a book on modesty by David and Diane Vaughn titled: "The Beauty of Modesty: Cultivating Virtue in the Face of a Vulgar Culture" (Nashville: Candlewick

Press, 2005), 103-105.

'A YCW must endeavour to be modest in the choice of her words. What she speaks; how it is spoken; and to whom it is spoken, are three considerations relative to modesty. Dirty jokes, as they are called, are not funny and should not be heard from the mouth of a YCW. Anything inappropriate should be avoided, especially when in mixed company, this is so that she represents Christ well and maturely. She has a duty to endeavour to make sure that she suggests nothing impure, sensual, or base. All that she says should have the aroma of grace and gratefulness upon it. 'And whatever you do in word or deed, do all in the name of the Lord Jesus, giving thanks to God the Father through Him' (Colossians 3:17). If what she has to say could not be spoken in God's presence, it is better left unsaid. When it comes to modest speech, there are two general rules a YCW should consider one of which is, think before she speaks. She needs to remember, words are like plucked feathers. Once cast to the breeze they can't be mended. Secondly, intimate matters should stay at home; a man and a woman who are not married 'should avoid talking about intimate subjects. They can discuss politics, art, business, or sports. However, they should avoid topics that may initiate or strengthen feelings of sexuality.'

Chapter 14

Modesty (Part 2)

A young Christian woman should also be modest in her character as that is what defines her. It's what people see in her. It's what people will say about her after she passes away. Character is one of the most important things a woman has. It is crucial that she is investing in building her character in a way that is pleasing to God and makes God famous. People should be able to see her faith demonstrated through her character. Her character will be reflected in how she serves the members of the body of Christ that she finds herself with. When a woman is being modest in her character, she is being considerate and meek. Humility is KEY here, a humble character is so important; scripture says a broken heart and contrite spirit the

Lord will not despise (Psalm 51:17).

Being modest (humble) also goes for the home (Colossians 3:18-21), in the community (Colossians 4:5), and in the congregation (Ephesians 4:16).

Elders are also expected to be Modest in Behaviour. A woman doesn't have to have grey hair to be considered an elder. An elder in the early church was someone mature in the faith and who had a leadership role. So if a young woman holds a leadership role, modest behaviour is also expected of her.

Furthermore, her life should be well-behaved, orderly, and moderate and dignified (Titus 2:2). Also in her home, even if she is not married and does not have children and she probably holds no position other than the last born in the family, it is important that she demonstrates moderate behaviour (1 Tim 3:4-5).

Moderate behaviour does not mean being quiet all the time and downplaying your personality. No.

it's about self-control and discipline; knowing when to speak and when to remain quiet; understanding that even if you are right, you don't have to defend yourself for the sake of peace.

1 Timothy 4:12 says, **Let no man despise thy youth; but be thou an example of the believers, in word, in conversation, in charity, in spirit, in faith, in purity.** Titus 2:7 - **In all things shewing thyself a pattern of good works: in doctrine [shewing] incorruptness, gravity, sincerity, Also In the community you should be blameless (1 Timothy 3:2, 1 Peter 3:15-16.) and also in the congregation you are is steadfast and faithful. (Hebrew 13:7.)**

Modesty in Material things

We all desire the good things of life and we all want to enjoy life. That's fully understandable, but as Christians we can sometimes get carried away with the fact that this place isn't our home, eternity is. We begin to idolise the things that scripture says are temporal, will perish and pass away (2 Corinthians 4:18). These things are distractions and they come from us not fixing our gaze on God.

The main scripture that comes to mind in regards to material modesty is Mark 8:36

And what do you benefit if you gain the whole world but lose your own soul? ... For what does it profit a man to gain the whole world and forfeit his soul?

This scripture makes it clear that gathering all the "wonderful" things of this world will not do a young woman any benefit. I am not saying that God encourages poverty, no. Jeremiah 29:11 shows that God does want her to prosper but he also desires that she does not idolise these things above Him. He should be her ONLY idol. To keep herself in check from time to time, a young woman should think about the things she loves and by the guidance of the holy spirit ask Him to reveal that which have become idols. She should then ask God to help her dethrone them and place Him upon the throne of her heart.

With regards to clothes, material modesty is not anti-beautiful or anti-handsome. Being modest does not mean that a young woman cannot look cute and lovely or that she is restricted from expressing her sense of style. However, it's about doing it in a way that expresses humility. At the outset, we should take note that Paul is not anti-adornment. The force of his statement is positive: "women should adorn themselves." The same word "adorn" is used to speak of a bride beautifying herself for her husband (Revelation 21:2). It is a term that expresses being ornamented, well-kempt, and put in order. The question for Paul isn't about whether a woman should ornament her body, but how she should do it. While the Bible only specifically addresses the need for women to dress modestly, the same teaching would apply to men in principle. Both men and women should bring glory to God in their manner of dress.

Modesty in the way a woman dresses is not just for church; but to be the standard for all Christians at all times. The key to understanding what constitutes modesty in dress is to examine the attitudes and intents of the heart. Those whose hearts are inclined toward God will make every effort to dress modestly, decently, and appropriately. Those whose hearts are inclined toward self will dress in a manner designed to draw attention to themselves with little or no regard for the consequences to themselves or others.

Modesty is about who a young woman worships. Scripture says your treasure is where your heart is (Matthew 6:21). A young woman will not only view modesty as an exterior thing but a thing of the heart. She will seek to please where her heart is. If her heart is with the Lord she will delight in him and make sure that she does ALL to please Him and make Him known.

In Ephesus, the original destination of this letter (1 Timothy 2:9), the cultural elite were known for their gaudy and extravagant wardrobes, their elaborate hair styles, and their expensive clothing that communicated extraordinary wealth. Paul paints a picture of this for the Ephesian Christians and says, "Don't mimic that. When you come to church, come dressed in a way that shows you desire the attention to be on God, not yourself."

A young woman's manner of dress, or even her preoccupation with clothing itself (Matthew 6:28-30), is often indicative of a heart that loves self-more than God. Modesty involves cultural discretion. A lack of discretion can result to misinterpretation and the introduction of rules and regulations which can in turn suffocate a young woman rather than liberate her. Paul didn't just generalise when talking about modesty; he gave details. He said braided hair and gold or pearls or costly attire were out of place for a truly modest woman. Some knowledge of Roman culture is helpful in understanding what Paul was saying. In Paul's day, Greek hairstyles for women were fairly simple: hair was parted in the middle and pinned in the back. But a culture change was sweeping the region. Women in the majestic household were wearing their hair with elaborate curls and braids, covered in expensive ornaments. The elite throughout the empire copied this style. For Paul, the appearance of braids and ornaments was more about what the fashion communicated. They carried connotations of imperial luxury and conjured up images of notoriously immoral Empresses like Valeria Messalina and Poppeaea Sabina; ancient equivalents of Cosmopolitan cover girls.

The poet Juvenal, a contemporary of Paul, gives

a vivid description of this cultural trend:

"There is nothing that a woman will not permit herself to do; nothing that she deems shameful. And when she encircles her neck with green emeralds and fastens huge pearls to her elongated ears, so important is the business of beautification. So numerous are the tiers and stories piled one another on her head that she pays no attention to her own husband."

Similarly, the philosopher Philo gives a description of a prostitute in his writing called "The Sacrifices of Cain and Abel":

"A prostitute is often described as having hair dressed in elaborate braids, her eyes with pencil lines, her eyebrows smothered in paint and her expensive clothes embroidered lavishly with flowers and bracelets and necklaces of gold and jewels hanging all over her."

Paul's description of immodest dress conjured a picture of someone preoccupied with appearance, fashion, luxury, and sexual prowess. Similarly, modern modesty standards are not about arbitrary rules of how much skin is shown or how low-cut something is, but about the messages and values our clothing communicates."

Modesty is about true freedom, not repression. More often than not, modesty standards are seen as repressive, arbitrary rules that restrict creativity and freedom. But when modesty is motivated from the heart, the exact opposite is true.

Self-control might be better understood as "self-mastery," being of sound mind or sober, being in control of one's impulses and appetites. In extra-biblical literature, this word has sexual nuances: being able to totally control your romantic and erotic desires.

Immodesty is often, though not always, a kind of slavery. People are enslaved by their desire to attract the opposite. They now define themselves by their fashion sense, their sex appeal, their image, their weight, or the brand names they wear. This kind of slavery is widespread because sin impacts us all, and in today's sexually charged, media-saturated culture, many women fall prey to this kind of slavery. But as Christians we are free from the slavery of sin because we are united in Christ. Paul exhorts us to live out this freedom: "Let not sin therefore reign in your mortal body, to make you obey its passions" (Romans 6:12). When it comes to modest dress, we can follow Paul's next statement quite literally: **Do not present the members of your body to sin as instruments for unrighteousness, but present your members to God as instruments for righteousness** (v.13). Paul wants Christians to have self-mastery in their wardrobe choices, to be totally free from worldly ways of defining worth, good looks, and sexiness.

Ironically, it is not just those who are scantily dressed that are enslaved, but even those who pride themselves on their modesty. "Modest is hottest," they say, unaware that in their own hearts, they are still enslaved to a preoccupation with their physical image, still defining their worth by their outward adornment.

When it comes to the subject of modesty, the first question we should ask ourselves is: What am I trying to accomplish? What are my motives?

Chapter 15

Building Godly relationships

*B*uilding Godly relationships take time and effort. Now before your mind runs wild, when I talk about relationships I am not talking solely about romantic ones. I am also talking about friendships, mentorships etc. It is pivotal that a YCW's relationships are God-centred. Her friendships should not be like the world's, neither should her romantic relationships. In fact, every intimate relationship she has should be based on sacrifice and love. When Christ walked on earth, He did not have that many intimate relationships apart from His disciples and even amongst them he had the ones with whom he was most intimate, James, John and Peter. However, we know that he was very sacrificial in his dealings with them and loved them throughout their time with Him on earth.

It is a difficult task to love and to be sacrificial, but that's why we have Christ and the Holy Spirit to help mould our hearts that we are able to love. Scripture says that we love because He loved us first. Now, when building godly relationships, there are many factors that have to be considered. The type of relationship it is, the people involved in the relationship and the purpose of the relationship. Many times when a YCW starts to form a relationship she is not cautious and this can lead to many things such as hurt, heartbreak, betrayal etc. This is not what God desires for her. He desires that her relationships with his other children are not toxic to her and to the other party. There are many types of relationships a Godly young woman will probably build in her lifetime. These are mentee-ships, mentorships, friendships, family, casual (acquaintances), and romantic relationships.

As a woman grows through the different stages of womanhood, her relationships will change; sometimes drastically and sometimes not so much. She needs to understand the different relationships in her life and the purpose that they serve. I would say that there are two key relationships in a young woman's life that will always evolve. However, these relationships can either make or break her. She can learn a lot from them or lose a lot.

#1 – Mentee-ship

The definition of a mentor is someone who is a wise AND TRUSTED counsellor or teacher. Discernment is fundamental to develop this kind or relationship with someone. This is a relationship that involves an individual willingly subjecting themselves to the teachings and guidance of another. As a younger woman it is imperative that you seek out mentors. Those who will guide you and give you sound biblical advice. Those who will see you through the hard times of life and be there to encourage you and teach you how to get through it. For a younger woman it is ideal to seek out a godly older woman. I had earlier explained the qualities of a Godly older woman. Every young woman should have an older woman similar to that in her life that she can speak to and look to for advice and nurturing.

Children cannot be left alone in a kitchen. There are many tools in there that they can use to hurt themselves if they don't know how to use them properly, so adult supervision is needed. As a young woman is growing through life, there are many hassles and disturbances that come with growing up and she will need someone to be there to hold her hand through the process. Attempting to do it herself, will lead to unnecessary and sometimes costly mistakes. It reminds me of one of the letters written in one of the previous chapters. The young woman expressed that she wouldn't have made some mistakes she made if the older woman in her life did her job. It's understandable if the older woman in a young woman's life is not necessarily doing her job, it is the job of the younger woman to seek out another. She should ask the Lord to lead her to the person that will do this job well.

Many times young women do not want to be accountable. This culture encourages exclusivity and isolation and we know that scripture says in Proverbs 18:1-2

1 A man who isolates himself seeks his own desire; He rages against all wise judgment. 2 A fool has no delight in understanding, But in expressing his own heart.

When a young woman isolates herself from others and from mentorship and guidance, scripture say she seeks her own desires. This means she seeks to do that which she believes is right. Scripture says that the heart of man is desperately wicked, so that means our heart naturally seeks to do wickedness. So when a young woman refuses to make herself accountable to mentors or those in leadership over her, she not only rages against all wise judgement but also wants to express the wickedness of her heart.

#2- Friendships

Right, so this part is so deep! There are many things that I have seen and heard about friendships that could have been avoided. We find Solomon's classic exposition on the value of friendship in Ecclesiastes 4:9-12:

Two are better than one, because they have a good reward for their labour. For if they fall, one will lift up his companion. But woe to him who is alone when he falls, for he has no one to help him up. Again, if two lie down together, they will keep warm; but how can one be warm alone? Though one may be overpowered by another, two

can withstand him. And a threefold cord is not quickly broken.

The last sentence of the passage refers to a three-fold cord. If one individual and another individual make a twofold cord, the threefold cord must have an additional element that we can infer to be God Almighty. If God is not placed first in every relation-ship that we human beings make (marriage, friend-ship, or church fellowship) the relationship will be momentary. Many young women often forget this and try to build two fold friendships. The third cord is the tie that binds the other two cords together.

The two cord friendship… This is a type of friendship that does not have God as its foundation. It's true that sometimes friendships don't start off with God being the tie that binds and can then turn into wonderful friendships. However the beauty of this relationship will have no eternal significance. If we are to be eternally minded as believers then our friendships should be eternally minded. A strong Christian friendship blossoms naturally when two friends grow together in faith, goodness, knowledge, and other godly graces.

A two fold friendship lacks selflessness. There are constant fights and disagreements. There's betrayal and there's conceit, there's no peace. It's possible to have relationships without quarrels but lacking peace. Peace is the absence of fear and weariness of soul. The attack of a wilful disposition is what causes weariness in the relationships that people have. This means that if a friendship attacks a young woman's personality and makes her feel less than adequate, she needs to flee as soon as she can. This is an unsafe place to be. A two cord friendship does not understand sacrifice and love. The young woman involved in a two-fold friendship might find it hard to leave the relationship because it can easily become manipulative. There's no 'freedom' in this relationship and there's no consistency or depth.

Anything built on hypothesis/suppositions will ultimately crash under the force of ignorance. Ignorance can be classified as a subconscious force that causes a person to sink. If a young woman's friendship is founded on gossip or mutual pain or pride, it will not be of benefit to either her or her friend. Sometimes a woman might forget what founded her friendships, she needs to make sure that she reviews her friendships often. The maintenance of friendships remind me of this scripture in 1 Corinthians 10:12

Therefore let him who thinks he stands take heed lest he fall

When this is applied to friendships, the participants have to make sure that they are taking all precautions to makes sure that even though the friendship is standing, they should give careful attention to their friendships by cultivating it and checking the foundations so that they are smooth and nothing is being missed that could cause a loss of gravity.

Chapter 16

The three-fold cord relationship

*T*he three-fold friendship is one of sacrificial love, acceptance, trust, respect for boundaries, and mutual edification.

#1 sacrificial love

John 15:13

Greater love has no one than this that he lay down his life for his friends. (NIV)

When a young woman wants to look into an example of friendship, Jesus is the ultimate example of a true Christian friend. His love for her is sacrificial; he is never selfish. He demonstrated it not only through his miracles of healing, but more fully through the humble service of washing the disciples' feet, and then ultimately, when he laid down his life on the cross. If a woman chooses her friends based only on what they have to offer, she will not be able to discover the blessings and beauty of a genuine friendship. In Philippians 2:3 says, **"Do nothing out of selfish ambition or vain conceit, but in humility consider others better than yourselves."** In this scripture we see that it is a requirement for her to put her friend's needs above hers. This way she is not only displaying agape love but she's then able to even come into greater and deeper understanding of God's love. There's beauty in serving others and laying her needs below theirs, there's this beautiful fulfilment that comes from it. She'll be on her way to loving like Jesus. In the process, she'll likely gain a true friend. A young woman should demonstrate sacrificial love in ways that the person does not even have to notice, but Abba. Things like praying for them in your secret place without them asking.

#2 Acceptance

Proverbs 17:17 - **A friend loves at all times, and a brother is born for adversity. (NIV)**

A young woman will discover the best of friendships with people who know and accept her weaknesses and imperfections. If a young woman is easily offended or holds on to bitterness, she'll have a hard time making meaningful friends. As a Christian, it is important that she allows the Holy Spirit to work on her heart. Forgiveness is not easy and it's true it can be hard and daunting but it's truly a beautiful thing. I'll share something that one of my brothers in Christ wrote about forgiveness. His name is Michael Olasope (Founder and CEO of the Vermin Campaign)

"Forgiveness isn't for them, it's for you." Another very inspirational but unbiblical statement accepted by so many believers, that has no root in the Word of God.

It's good, but not God. There is no true forgiveness without agape love. However in John 15:12, we are COMMANDED to love as Jesus loves. As God loves. In John 3:16, we see that God gave the son for US.

That WE may no longer be condemned His forgiveness was for us.

Philippians 2:3 calls us to think of others more highly than ourselves. To choose to forgive them just for ourselves, is selfish and no longer comes out of a heart of love. Another problem is, if it's just for ourselves, it's easier to hold un-forgiveness. It's like, I'm the one suffering. I can handle it. If we truly loved the brethren (evidence of salvation), then it would be hard to keep un-forgiveness, cause we then realise how much it harms them. We keep them to their past. No matter how they want to grow and change, their guilt is held against them. God was justified in his anger against us and sin, yet he was more focused on restoring us!

Romans 12:20 and Proverbs 25:22 show us that helping our enemies is for them. It says as we love and forgive those who hurt us, we heap coals of fire upon them. However, symbolically a coal of fire is a purifying agent (Isaiah 6:7), not a weapon.

If we're going to look at it biblically, forgiveness is more for them, than us. You say "what if they don't deserve it". I say, because I did not accept the blood of Christ in my youth, why didn't Christ "cancel" his sacrifice and forgiveness?

Don't get me wrong. We benefit greatly. Every single commandment God gives us benefits us in the long run. However, if the Bible says love is selfless, then forgiveness must be selfless as well. No wonder Phillipians 2:3 first calls us to be humble before thinking of others more highly. Because pride makes you think more about how you feel, than the other person. Sorry if this hurts, but it's not about YOU. Be careful of inspirational statements that have no root in God's Word. Let's search out the scripture.

From this, a young woman can see that no one is perfect as she and many others will make mistakes now and then. It's important that she takes a truthful look at herself to make sure that the failure of the relationship was not just the other party but that she sees where she has gone wring so she can rectify things with the friend and not make the same mistake again. Sometimes we end up bearing some of the blame when things go wrong in a friendship. A good friend is quick to ask forgiveness and ready to be forgiving.

#3 Ample Trust

Proverbs 18:24

A man of many companions may come to ruin, but there is a friend who sticks closer than a brother. (NIV)

This proverbs has a lot of depth to it. It reveals that a true Christian friend is dependable, indeed, but accentuates another vital truth as well. A Christian woman should only expect to share complete trust with a limited number of steadfast friends. It is true that we are to love everyone but there is something that I personally do when it comes to choosing my friends. Firstly, a woman has to understand that just as she chooses her husband she can also choose her friends. Proverbs 14:6-7 says, **a scoffer seeks wisdom and finds none, but knowledge is easy to one who has understanding. Leave the presence of a fool, or you will not discern words of knowledge.**

This scripture shows that a person needs to leave the presence of a fool: someone who can be classified as a counterfeit. A young woman does not need counterfeit relationships in her life. So the first step is choosing to leave the presence of a counterfeit. After this she then asks the Lord to guide her and open her eyes to see the originals around her. As a young woman, trusting too easily can lead to loss, so be careful about putting your confidence in a mere companion. Every relationship will be tested and tried and anything that stands in the fire will come out as fine as gold. Over time her true friends will prove their trustworthiness by sticking closer than a brother or sister.

#4 Strong Boundaries

1 Corinthians 13:4

Love is patient, love is kind. It does not envy ... (NIV)

If a woman feels overpowered in a friendship, something is wrong. This is because she might be in an indirect mentorship relationship and this might not fulfil her need for mutual friendship. Therefore, the relationship might seem draining and overwhelming. Likewise, if she feels used or abused, something is incorrect; a friendship like that is suffocating. It makes her feel like she cannot leave or make new friends. If her friend gets angry easily or becomes too jealous when she makes new friends then she should be cautious and discuss these worries with her friend. Similarly, a woman should recognize what's best for her and the other person, and from there, giving that person space are signs of a healthy relationship. A true friendship will wisely avoid intruding and recognize each other's need to maintain other relationships.

#5 Reciprocated Edification

Proverbs 27:6

Wounds from a friend can be trusted ... (NIV)

This scripture is packed with truth. Women in intimate friendships should be able to build each other up emotionally, spiritually, and physically. Friends like to be together simply because it feels good. In a woman's friendships, there should be a mutual drawing of strength, encouragement and love. They should be able to talk to each other sincerely, cry with each other and listen to each other.

On the other hand though, it is important that a young woman says and hears the difficult things her dearest friend needs to say or hear. Yet, in many friendships this is what is lacking, the hard truth.

Friends no longer tell each other the truth but now they mask it. If a young woman is hesitant in correcting her friend, then there is something wrong in that relationship. When two people have shared trust and acceptance, there's respect for each other but most importantly deep care to see the other person do well and on the right path. As a young woman, her words should be said with love especially when she's correcting a sensitive part of her friend's heart. For she is the only one that knows how to deliver the hard message with truth and grace. I believe this is what Proverbs 27:17 means when it says, "As iron sharpens iron, so one man sharpens another."

Hopefully, these examples of a three-fold friendship have highlighted some areas that may need a little work in a young woman's determination to build stronger friendships. She should not be disheartened if she does not have that many close friends but should make it a priority to strengthen the ones she might already have. She needs to remember that true Christian friendships are rare treasures. They take time to nurture, but in the process we grow more Christ like

RIPE

One and only Chapter

The section of this book will be quite different. To be quite honest it has been the HARDEST part of the book to write. This is because with this stage in a woman's life and her maturity in womanhood, there are many things that can come as a distraction. Women across the body of Christ have very different lives wherever they may be but one thing that joins us together is Jesus Christ and out love for Him. In this stage of a woman's life there are many things probably running through her head. Such as being financially independent, marriage, ministry, her children, her home, her business etc. So many things and one thing that I believe is important to keeping sanity in her mind is the hope she has in Jesus Christ. In this section I will be brief and concise and I will discuss two things: Simplicity and Focus. When we look at the word ripe, it means arriving at a stage of growth or development as to be ready for reaping, gathering, eating, or use as GRAIN or fruit; completely matured. I found this definition interesting especially the use of the word grain. This is because the word grain is also seed. I'll expand in a bit.

A woman gets to her ripe age when she is completely matured in her spirit. This can also happen if she submits herself to the guidance of the Holy Spirit and obeys the Lord fervently. When something is ripe, it is very likely that it can rot. This is not what we want but when this thing that is ripe is put back into the ground, it is able to produce more.

Simplicity is one thing that we miss as women. When a woman ripens she's to get simpler. Not in the sense that she becomes dull and foolish but that she has less distractions and one ultimate goal, where she understands that all her trials and tribulations are working for one grand plan. When she is focused she will be able sow correctly to see more fruit. Simplicity and focus work hand in hand. Where there is freedom from complexity, intricacy, or division there is focus and focus brings the change you want to see. From time to time, Jesus had to remind his disciples that he will be leaving; he was about his Father's business. He had focus. He did not get wrapped up in what was going on around Him. For example, in the way His disciples felt, the wrong accusations, the bonds that he had created on earth. He saw the end goal of his mission on earth and he already started to prepare himself long before the kiss of Judas. He focused on that and even when He got weary, He said "let your will be done, Lord".

There are so many issues surrounding women in the body of Christ and sometimes these can cause us to lose focus on the most important things which are Jesus, the cross, and eternity. When, as women, we focus on these things more and pray about them rather than engaging in futile discussions, we will change and see it manifested in our spheres of influence. I see very little conferences for women to simply pray for their families, communities, businesses, towns and nations. There are more conferences on things such as modesty, singleness, courtships etc., please do not get me wrong! These things are excellent and needed but we have raised them above being women of prayer. Oh, if only our women prayed as fervently as they went to these conferences and discussed these issues. There are so any conflicting opinions that we have forgotten that we are to be like children to enter Kingdom of God.

Mathew 18:3

And said, Verily I say unto you, except ye be converted, and become as little children, ye shall not enter into the kingdom of heaven

This scripture shows that it takes action and willingness to be like a child. It says be converted the word there in Greek is 'strepho'. This word means to twist, we know that twisting takes longer than just turning (accepting Jesus, justification). The twisting is the converting of a person's soul, where the word is renewing their mind, causing them to submit their will, stabilising their emotions and sitting on the throne of their heart. Then they have to become like children. To some it might be like 'but that's digression'. No it's not. It's actually, humbling yourself, just like Jesus did so that we may be reconciled with God. He had gone through the twisting and it was even solidified when he said Lord thy will and not mine, Luke 22:42

"Father, if you are willing, take this cup from me; yet not my will, but yours be done."

This was a place of perfect strength and perfect weakness. That's what Mathew 18:3 encourages. Being so twisted (converted) but still so weak (a child).

When a woman gets to this stage and begins to walk in His will, she is then able to produce Christ in others through the help of the Holy Spirit. She now becomes a grain (a child) and she's able to not only enter the kingdom but also bring her friends (her fruit).

John 12:24

Very truly I tell you, unless a kernel of wheat falls to the ground and dies, it remains only a single seed. But if it dies, it produces many seeds

I have left this section short because this is what the Holy Spirit wanted. So take time to dissect what you have just read and ask the Holy Spirit to teach you more.

Father, thank you for creating me as a woman, I am thankful that you have graced me with the gift to internalise.

Thank you for creating me with qualities that
aid the advancement of humanity.
Thank you for the woman I was, I am,
and will be.
Thank you that I am growing from glory to
glory. I love your work in me, and
I will forever love you my bridegroom.
Take all the glory Jesus.
I cannot wait to see you x

The End